KU-425-514

MODERN THEOLOGY
2. Rudolf Bultmann

MODERN THEOLOGY

Selections from twentieth-century theologians
edited with an introduction and notes by

E. J. TINSLEY

2
Rudolf Bultmann

1884–

LONDON

EPWORTH PRESS

© E. J. Tinsley 1973

First published 1973
by Epworth Press
All rights reserved
No part of this publication
may be reproduced, stored in a
retrieval system, or
transmitted, in any form or by
any means, electronic, mechanical,
photocopying, recording or
otherwise, without the prior
permission of Epworth Press

Enquiries should be addressed to
The Methodist Publishing House
The Book Room
2 Chester House
Muswell Hill
London N10 1PZ

SBN 7162 0216 6

Printed in Great Britain by
The Garden City Press Limited
Letchworth, Hertfordshire
SG6 1JS

ACKNOWLEDGEMENTS

The author and publisher are grateful for permission to quote in this series from the following works:

Church Dogmatics, Vol. I, 2; IV, 2, T. and T. Clark
Deliverance to the Captives, by Karl Barth, SCM Press
Kerygma and Myth, Vol. I; II, edited by H. W. Bartsch, SPCK
Christology, by Dietrich Bonhoeffer, Collins Publishers
Ethics, by Dietrich Bonhoeffer, SCM Press
Letters and Papers from Prison, by Dietrich Bonhoeffer, SCM Press
Sanctorum Communio, by Dietrich Bonhoeffer, Collins Publishers
The Cost of Discipleship, by Dietrich Bonhoeffer, SCM Press
Form Criticism, by Bultmann and Kundsin, Harper and Row, New York
Theology of the New Testament, Vol. II, by Rudolf Bultmann, translated by F. Grobel, SCM Press
Word and Faith, by G. Ebeling, translated by J. W. Leitch, SCM Press
The Nature of Faith, by Gerhard Ebeling, Collins Publishers
Selections from Karl Barth's Church Dogmatics, by H. Gollwitzer, T. and T. Clark
The Systematic Theology of Paul Tillich, by A. J. McKelway, Lutterworth Press
Beyond Tragedy, by Reinhold Niebuhr, James Nisbet and Co. Ltd
Leaves from the Notebook of a Tamed Cynic, by Reinhold Niebuhr, Harper and Row, New York
The Nature and Destiny of Man, Vol. I; II, by Reinhold Niebuhr, James Nisbet and Co. Ltd
World Come of Age, edited by R. Gregor Smith, Collins Publishers
The Death of God, by Gabriel Vahanian, George Braziller, Inc., New York

CONTENTS

PREFACE TO THE SERIES

The theologians represented in this series of five volumes of selections are those who, one can confidently say, are already assured of an important place in the history of twentieth-century theology.

In the case of each theologian I have tried to give a fair representation of the author's work although, inevitably, there are important aspects of his thought which I have not always found it possible to illustrate. I have throughout preferred to give substantial selections rather than short extracts because the qualities of the writing of the theologians in this collection require this treatment for proper understanding and illustration. Even so selections are no substitute for the original, and it is my hope that readers will become sufficiently interested in what is given in this series to want to go to the full range of the authors' complete works.

As well as being representative of an influential group of theologians I hope that the selections provided will be found to provide something of an integrated discussion among the writers themselves. I have, therefore, in making the selections included some which give an idea how these theologians view each other. The reader is given some indication of the views, say, of Barth on Bultmann or Niebuhr on Barth, and there are cross-references in the introduction and notes so that he can have an idea of what subjects have been of continuing importance in modern theological discussion.

I have made this selection not only for those who have a professional interest in the study of theology (clergy and ministers, teachers, students) but also for the interested member of the general public who, whether believer or not, wishes to have a guide to a reading of some important phases of twentieth-century theology. A general introduction attempts to set the scene and for each author there is a biographical note and brief introductions to the selected passages. In each case also there are suggestions for further study and reading.

University of Leeds   JOHN TINSLEY

INTRODUCTION TO THE SERIES

In this introductory chapter an attempt will be made to explain how the present theological situation in western Europe and the United States has come about. We shall trace very briefly the pedigree of contemporary ideas and attitudes. 'Theology' however is a word (like, e.g., 'mysticism', 'romanticism', 'philosophy') which is frequently and easily used without its meaning having first been made clear. It is not uncommon to find politicians and other public speakers using the word 'theology' to mean some recondite, antiquarian and hopelessly irrelevant intellectual pursuit involving, it is implied, a sad waste of mental energy. It is essential therefore to try first to clarify the meaning of the term 'theology'. A good way of doing this is to describe how theology is done. By describing the process of theology we shall more easily come to an understanding of what it essentially is.

Perhaps there have been as many attempts at a definition of theology as, for example, of art. The comparison with art is very relevant because theology is in one aspect, and a very important one, an instance of the perennial task of working with words to achieve lucidity and precision described by T. S. Eliot as 'the intolerable wrestle with words and meanings'. Even if we think we have found a more or less satisfactory language very often the cultural situation will have meantime so moved on that we find, in Eliot's words again, that we have only learned to get better words for the things we no longer want to say.

Nevertheless theologians have to keep on with this task not because they believe that it is possible, for instance, to describe 'God' or to find a language about God which is valid for all time, but because they believe that theology is a perennial human task. Man is a 'theologizing' animal: i.e., he must be constantly attempting to achieve in a significant pattern of words (or of words together with gestures and sound, as, for example, in liturgy) some way of rationalizing all those facets of his experience and history which point to a meaning beyond the visible and material. Because the most significant activity in religion, worship, involves among other things a particular use of language theology is, whether the fact be acknowledged by theologians or not, vitally linked with the arts and the problems raised by artistic creativity. Hence the amount of space taken up in this book with discussion of the nature of religious language, and the use of symbol, myth and metaphor in religion.

These subjects are of common interest to theologians and students of literature, and of the arts in general. The question of theology and language is however of special concern to the *Christian* theologian and the reason for this has never been better expressed than by St Augustine. In a famous passage in his *De Trinitate* he discusses the question why Christians should use trinitarian language when speaking about God. He is aware of the irritation and impatience of those who feel that theological language is attempting to make definitions precisely in a sphere where, in the nature of the case, such a thing is not possible. Augustine replies, however, that Christians have to be careful about language, especially language about God, *non ut diceretur sed ne taceretur*, which could be paraphrased 'not in order to define but because it is not possible just to say nothing'. Christians, of all people, cannot keep silence, adds Augustine, because God has broken silence in Christ and has spoken to mankind in him. We are bound therefore to make the best reply that we can.

More particularly theology invites comparison with what may properly be called the art of criticism, since it has the same relation to its subject matter (religion) as, for example, music criticism has to the symphony, art criticism to painting or sculpture, or literary criticism to poetry or prose. The best theology, like the best art, is that which so uses language that it sends the reader back with new and fruitful perspectives to the original (e.g., Christ, the Bible, etc.), or so speaks of the original that it affords a fresh and creative present experience of it.

Perhaps because of the great variety of approaches and methods possible for doing theology it is better, and here again the analogy from art is useful, not to think of what theology may be in the abstract but of actual types and styles of theology, and it is hoped that the selections given in this book will enable the reader to do this. The types and styles of theology are analogous to the types and styles of art. One could readily think in theology of the equivalents of, say, representational, impressionist, expressionist or abstract art. The 'quest of the historical Jesus' in the nineteenth century bears a resemblance to the 'pre-Raphaelite' school of painting in its attempt to portray Jesus in full and minute detail. Rudolf Bultmann and the 'existentialist' school of modern theology remind one of German 'expressionist' art where the subject of the painting is used as a means of expressing the commitment, feeling and attitudes of the artist. Further, like styles in art, theological styles continue to have significance even though they belong to an age now long past. The artist and the theologian are both in constant dialogue with their past traditions. To be a genuine contemporary, in both fields, means to have lived through, in imaginative experience, the outlook of previous practitioners. Theology belongs to the realm of human creativity and is therefore a dynamic and changing phenomenon. It is better, therefore, at the beginning of one's study of such a subject to look at the various methods of doing theology rather than to seek some distillation of it, some quintessential theology.

It would not be difficult to say something about what theology is from an analysis of the two words which make up the term theology—'theos' and 'logos'. Starting from these two components we might translate 'theology' as 'God-talk'. Theology as 'God-talk' takes its origin from two permanent features of human existence. There is first the fact that from time to time, in all sorts of ways, man finds himself wondering whether there is any meaning to his existence, whether the values and ideals which strike him in a cogent way in his many moral and aesthetic experiences are anything more than fine moments of feeling. There is further an impatience and a restlessness about human existence—we long for serenity, for wholeness and harmony, for unity and purpose, and continue to wonder whether in and behind material existence there is another order of reality.

These intimations of something beyond time and space have been variously expressed whether in the classical scheme of the values of 'truth, beauty and goodness', or in what Rudolf

Otto[1] has called the experience of the 'holy' or the 'numinous', or as far as aesthetic experience is concerned, in what Longinus[2] called the 'sublime'. Others have used the term 'mystery' for these features of human existence to express their sense of that which is mysterious, not in the way of a puzzle which is in principle solvable at some time or other, but as inducing, rather than the desire to solve, an overwhelming impression of awe, wonder, reverence, joy.

For the centre of this 'mystery' the Greek word would have been *theos*, sometimes translated 'god', but we may conveniently use it for any kind of transcendental reference given to human life. Man is a being who finds it difficult to undergo artistic, religious, scientific or moral experience and leave it just like that. He finds himself involved necessarily in the task of shaping this experience into significant patterns, trying to hold it in words or in some visual form. More particularly he is prompted to speech about it, to try and contain this experience in sentences. It is to this necessary use of language to analyse and explain *theos* that one can give the Greek word *logos*. Theology is, therefore, strictly speaking *theos-logos*— 'God-talk'. Theology results from the fact that on the one hand there is the 'mystery' and on the other the impulse to achieve understanding of it.

It is significant that many theologians have expressed a similar impatience with their task to that which we find in poets. We have already referred to Augustine and T. S. Eliot on the difficulties and frustrations of finding satisfactory words. This raises an important issue. Most frequently when we use the term 'theology' we think, inevitably and rightly, of verbal theology: that analysis of the 'mystery' of existence, that articulation of *theos* which can be done in words (*logos*). No doubt one would have to say that the best theology is that which approximates most closely to the character of its subject-matter. In the case of Christian theology this would mean the character of the Incarnation especially its 'signful', indirect, ambiguous, parabolic quality. Perhaps a more adequate kind of theology, a more satisfactory response to the *theos*, is that

[1] *The Idea of the Holy*, 1923.
[2] Cassius Longinus, Greek philosopher and critic of third century A.D., author of a treatise on literary criticism, *On the sublime*.

expressed in a concrete but non-verbal way in the arts, particularly the visual arts. If this is the case we ought to coin a new word for this reaction to *theos*. It would be a question not of *theos* and *logos* (=*verbal* theology) but of *theos* and *poiesis* ('making')—'theo-poetics'. The use of such a term as 'theo-poetics' would remind one of the saying of W. B. Yeats, specially appropriate to the Christian religion, that man cannot know the truth or express it in words. He can only *embody* (perhaps one could say 'incarnate') it. Even if we must continue to use the word 'theology' we need to think of it as a perennial attempt to *embody* human experience of *theos* rather than to translate it into some prose paraphrase.

This analysis of the meaning of the word 'theology' is a start, but it does not take us very far. We need to examine more closely how theologians have set about the task of 'God-talk', and the data which they have taken to be relevant. We must therefore turn now to a brief review of what theologians have been doing during the last two centuries. This will help us to understand the theological scene today, and to recognize more clearly some of the 'styles' being used by theologians at the present time.

1

A radical change came over the method of doing Christian theology in the eighteenth century. Up till then, broadly speaking, and certainly from the time when theology had been given its most comprehensive and systematic expression in the works of St Thomas Aquinas (*c*. 1225–74) the procedure had seemed must therefore turn now to a brief review of what theologians investigation had two main parts: (1) natural theology and (2) revealed theology.

To take the method of doing 'natural' theology first. It was thought possible to establish by the ordinary processes of human reasoning such great truths as the existence of God and the immortality of the soul. Furthermore the ordinary processes of argumentation could establish the truth of certain attributes of God, like his omnipotence and omnipresence. From the evidence provided by the natural world and human

existence it was possible to establish the existence of God by
'proofs'. The existence of God could be demonstrated by the
use of unaided human reason. This was a truth about God
open to any enquirer and could therefore rightly be called
'natural' theology.

'Revealed' theology was an important supplement to this. It
had two additional functions to those performed by natural
theology. First of all it conveyed again the truths of natural
theology but this time in a 'revealed' form (particularly in the
Christian scriptures) which could be readily and easily understood by those who were not able to follow rational argument.
Then, second, revealed theology presented truths which could
not be demonstrated by human reason, such as, for instance,
the trinitarian nature of God. The scriptures attested the
divinity of Christ by showing that he fulfilled Old Testament
prophecy and worked miracles. These were taken to be the
two foundations of belief in the authority of Christ. They
established his place in the Christian revelation.

There were thus two kinds of data at the disposal of the
theologian, natural theology and revealed theology, or to put
it shortly 'reason' and 'revelation'. From an investigation of
the book of nature and the book of scripture the theologian
could construct an integrated and systematic theology, like the
Summa Theologiae of St Thomas Aquinas. This was the
general pattern of Christian apologetics commonly accepted
until comparatively recently, and has remained the official view
of the matter in the Roman Catholic Church. This method of
doing theology was enshrined in William Paley's *View of the
Evidences of Christianity* (1794) which remained in use as a
text-book until as late as the beginning of the present century.
Various criticisms had been brought against this way of doing
theology before the advent of modern developments in philosophy, the sciences, and in biblical criticism. Reformation
theology in general was suspicious of the large claims made
by natural theology for the use of man's 'unaided' reason. Not
only did the Reformers insist on the fact that all reasoning
is undergirded by grace but they questioned whether one could
say that human reason, even when so supported, inevitably
attained the truths of natural theology. This seemed to them to
neglect the problem of 'fallen' human nature which is capable

of perverting and corrupting even the process of reasoning. During the eighteenth century the unsatisfactory character of this traditional approach to theology became clearer still. Many Christian apologists in this period tried to develop a natural theology not by reading off from the book of nature but by searching, so to speak, the book of man's inner experience. This seemed to show that there was among human beings a general religious sense which lay behind all formally organized religions. So-called 'revealed' theology was therefore taken to be simply a sophisticated articulation of this universal natural theology. In this way the distinction between natural and revealed theology was blurred, to say the least. Christianity, for example, was seen not as a blend of natural and revealed theology but a particular version of the universal feeling for religion. To quote from the title of a book by a famous eighteenth-century Deist, Matthew Tindal, it was as 'old as creation', nothing more than 'a republication of the religion of nature'.

More dramatic in their effects on the traditional scheme of theology, however, were the developments in scientific investigation and historical criticism which gathered momentum during the eighteenth century and continued apace throughout the nineteenth century.

2

Research in the natural sciences during the nineteenth century, especially in the fields of geology and biology, produced a picture of the origin of the universe and its evolution radically different from that suggested by a literal acceptance of the early chapters of Genesis with a universe created in six days and an Adam and Eve as the first human beings. *The Bridgewater Treatises* (1833–40) showed, among other things, that it was quite impossible, from the evidence already made available by geological research, to subscribe to the view that Creation could be exactly dated, as Archbishop Ussher[1] had

[1] James Ussher (1581–1656), Archbishop of Armagh, worked out a complete biblical chronology in his *Annales Veteris et Novi Testamenti*, and the dates given in this book were inserted in editions of the Authorised Version of the Bible from 1701 onwards.

suggested, in 4004 B.C. For those who had been brought up
on the idea that the Bible was itself the revelation of God,
giving infallible truth as a series of propositions, this sugges-
tion that the earth was millions rather than thousands of years
old came as quite a shock. As late as 1851 John Ruskin could
write: 'If only the geologists would let me alone, I could do
very well, but those dreadful hammers! I hear the clink of
them at the end of every cadence of the Bible verses.'

Following hard upon this shock came the news from the
field of biological research. Charles Darwin's *The Origin of
Species* was published in 1859 and his *The Descent of Man* in
1871. These made it clear not only that human life had evolved
from sub-human species but that the whole process had been
inconceivably longer than was generally supposed. Again for
those brought up on the view that the Bible was a monolithic
structure infallible on all subjects, including the science of
human origins, this came as a great blow.

These shocks from outside the sphere of the Bible coincided
with developments within biblical criticism which at the time
seemed to undermine still further the status of the Bible as
authoritative Scripture. As a result of literary and historical
study it was no longer possible to maintain that the biblical
literature was all of one kind, and all on the same level of
authority or 'inspiration'. To take the Bible as an infallible
oracle, to believe that in it the Word of God took print, was
now seen to violate the nature of the biblical literature itself
and to presuppose that the divine method of revelation is one
which imposes rather than elicits, 'explains' rather than indicates, and forces rather than persuades.

Faced with these developments there were three possible
reactions from Christian apologists. One could first simply
refuse to recognize that any change had taken place and to
carry on using the Bible as before, if anything hardening one's
ideas about its authority and inerrancy. This is the approach
which later on came to have the label 'fundamentalism'
attached to it. Or, secondly, the attempt could be made to
reconcile the new developments in knowledge with the traditional structure of theology. This was often taken to quite
fantastic lengths like, for example, suggesting that the real
significance of fossils in no way turned out to be a contradic-

tion of the traditional dating of creation since they had been placed there by God to test faith! Similarly one remembers the notorious attempts to reconcile evolution with the scheme of creation in Genesis. Since the psalmist says that one day in the sight of the Lord is as a thousand years, 'days' in the Genesis account does not mean twenty-four hours but whatever extended period of time may be necessary to fit the case! Or, thirdly, one could accept the findings of research and in the light of them discard previous views of, for example, biblical inerrancy and look entirely afresh at the whole concept of revelation and the nature of the biblical literature. It was this latter reaction that has come to be known as nineteenth-century liberalism. Its main features were as follows.

First, a suspicion of the traditional schemes of dogmatic theology, and an attempt to reconstruct Christian belief in a way which took into account historical criticism. This could be illustrated by new procedures in such areas as christology or the doctrine of the Church. The traditional belief about the Christ as true God and true man, with two natures divine and human, as expressed in the traditional formula of the Council of Chalcedon 451 was put on one side, and an attempt made to construct a way of believing in Christ taking into account the results of historical criticism of the gospels, particularly the growing conviction that the fourth gospel, which had been a principal source for the formulation of traditional christology, was so much later than the synoptic gospels and so much less historical that it ought not to be used again in this way. The enigmatical Christ of the synoptic gospels, only indirectly indicating the meaning of himself, became the basis for a 'kenotic' christology. That is to say it was emphasized that whatever else the Incarnation was it meant an act of self-giving on the part of God which involved sacrificial self-limitation. Or again one could take the doctrine of the Church, especially in its relation to Christ. In the light of biblical and historical criticism it was felt by many nineteenth-century scholars that the Christ of history, the genuine Jesus of Nazareth, was one thing, and the Christ of Church doctrine quite another. It seemed to be self-evident that the historical Christ could not have intended the Church as an institution, but rather that he was an outstanding Hebrew prophet who was concerned with brotherly love, justice, and the inestimable worth of the human soul.

The second characteristic of nineteenth-century liberalism was the use made of the category of evolution, provided by developments in the biological sciences. Human history was seen in terms of evolutionary progress. Mankind was seen to be, indubitably, on the march of progress. By the use of reason and the intellectual tools at his disposal man would be able to fashion a better future for himself. 'Sin', if the word were used at all, ought to be put in inverted commas and translated to mean imperfection or ignorance. 'Salvation' consequently ought to be thought of in terms of education and enlightenment. Such biblical concepts as 'the kingdom of God' ought similarly to be reinterpreted in terms of some kind of evolutionary progressivism.

Out of all this came some new principles for theological method and the data to be used by theology. The Bible remained as a principal source for the Christian theologian but it had to be used critically in the light of the findings of literary and historical investigation. The Bible also needed to be detached from its traditional interpretation in the church. In particular allegorization and typology were discarded as both inappropriate and irrelevant to such a critical use of the Bible. The book of the universe, nature, was also a source to be used, especially since it provided such a category of interpretation as evolutionary development. Finally there was increasing use of human experience as a source for theology. Nineteenth-century theology was greatly influenced by the work of Friedrich Schleiermacher (1768–1834) who considered the essence of the religious sentiment to be the feeling of absolute dependence and interpreted Christ as the supreme example of such dependence and 'God-consciousness'.

As far as relations with philosophy were concerned it has to be remembered that in the nineteenth century the task of philosophy was taken to be, principally, to provide a 'metaphysics', that is an all-embracing interpretation of the universe and human existence. The philosopher was one who concerned himself with what Tillich (see Vol. 3, pp. 73 ff.) called the 'ultimate questions of human existence'. The theologian's task was to keep on the look-out for philosophical schemes whose general outlook and vocabulary seemed to be particularly well-suited for the exposition of Christian beliefs. It was widely held during the nineteenth century, both on the Continent and in Britain, that such a congenial philosophical system had been found in the work of Friedrich Hegel (1770–1831). Hegel believed that existence could best be interpreted in terms of an evolutionary process, continually advancing from thesis to antithesis and fresh synthesis, whereby the Absolute Idea realized itself in ever more sharply focused ways. Adapting Christian trinitarian language he thought of the eternal Idea as God the Father. The eternal Idea as constantly passing from infinitude to finitude he thought of as God the Son. The Absolute Idea returning home, so to speak, enriched by this outgoing (Incarnation) he identified with the Christian God the Holy Spirit.

3

This was the background against which we can place all the theological movements represented in this series. Paul Tillich has described himself as a nineteenth-century figure, and certainly his concept of the relation between theology and philosophy as a 'correlation' (see Vol. 3 pp. 39 ff.) makes him very much more akin to the philosophy of the last century than to the analytical anti-metaphysical philosophy which has dominated the academic scene in twentieth-century Britain. Karl Barth's theological thinking began as a strong reaction against the liberal theology of the nineteenth-century and particularly its alliance with philosophies which he believed prevented the unique and distinctive features of the Christian religion from being clearly expressed. Bultmann took up the issues raised by the development of biblical criticism in the nineteenth century, particularly the question of the relation between the Jesus of history and the Christ of faith. Bonhoeffer in his early period shared Barth's reaction to nineteenth-century theology but later came to believe that a quite new situation faces the twentieth-century Christian and that Barth was of decreasing usefulness to such a person. Niebuhr's theology of politics and society is a deliberate reaction to a liberal theology which he believed had seriously underplayed the doctrines of sin and original sin and had placed an ultimate trust in human intelligence and virtue. We now need to examine more fully the place in the history of twentieth-century theology likely to be occupied by these five theologians.

All five of them were German or, in the case of Niebuhr, of German origin. As it happens they were also all of clerical or academic households. Further they all had experienced the age of Nazism and in most cases had suffered from it in one way or another.

The beginning of the theological movement associated with the name of *Karl Barth* can be dated from his shocked realization that the values of nineteenth-century liberalism as held by academics and intellectuals of his day left them incapable of recognizing tyranny when it appeared, much less of standing up against it. Academic education, even in theology, did not make men any more able to perceive the illiberalism and aggression implicit in the German policies which led to the outbreak of the 1914–18 war (see Vol. 1, pp. 36 ff.). The same inability of the liberal mind to believe in the recalcitrant and anti-rational possibilities of human conduct displayed itself again when the Nazis came to power in 1934. The theological charter which became the rallying point of church resistance to Hitler, the Barmen declaration, was mainly the work of Barth.

Certainly nothing could be more contrary to the theological method of nineteenth-century liberalism than that promulgated by Barth. For him the theological endeavour begins not with a series of questionings about human existence or the universe but by a realization that man is first confronted by an answer, a divine answer in the form of a revelation to which a unique witness is borne by the Bible. 'Religion' as the human enquiry after God, the human endeavour to attain God by the exercise of human reason is anathema to Barth (see Vol. 1, pp. 56 ff.). It is impossible for man to take any initiative, strictly speaking, in his enquiries about God because by his very existence man is a potential recipient of a revelation which is one of the inescapable givennesses of life. God is essentially a prevenient God who has first spoken to man, and anything that man says, any enquiry that he may make, must necessarily take the form of a response to a God who has all the while been addressing him. This is a method of doing theology directly opposed to that of Paul Tillich who begins his theology precisely with human questions, the 'ultimate questions' posed by human existence.

This starting point led Barth to place a new kind of emphasis on the Bible and the place of scripture in the formation of dogmatic theology. This started a movement which later on came to be known as 'biblical theology'. The Bible was regarded as providing the categories for Christian theology. Barth's theology has been given different names. One of them, his own term, is 'kerygmatic' theology, namely a theology which has first and foremost to be proclaimed. It is not sensible to argue about revelation Barth believed; one can only proclaim it.

There is also in Barth a new emphasis on the indissoluble links between theology and the church. Academic theology in the nineteenth century, especially in Germany, was separated from the life of the Church and the work of the pastor. The Church as the believing community came to have a new meaning for Barth as the body which finds itself bearing the Word of God and being judged by it.

Barth's way of doing Christology, of tackling the problems raised by the person of Christ, seems at first sight to be very much in the traditional manner. He began from the traditional formulation of the Council of Chalcedon of Christ as true God and true man. But he soon showed himself to be suspicious of the historical method of the nineteenth-century 'quest of the historical Jesus'. Barth suspected that this really made faith dependent on the results of historical investigation and practically equivalent to acceptance of an agreed amount of reliable factual information about Christ. It is instructive at this point to compare Barth's attitude to the historical Jesus with that of Bultmann, Tillich and Bonhoeffer. Barth treated more creatively and fruitfully than the nineteenth century the question of *kenosis* (self-emptying) in the Incarnation. This was not for Barth a matter of some loss of divinity, a downgrading of God. The *kenosis* in Christ is in fact the highest affirmation of the lordship of God over all. God is lord not only in transcendent glory but even in the form of the servant. God is free to be other personalities without ceasing to be himself. Whereas for so many 'kenotic' theologians in the nineteenth (and indeed twentieth centuries) the Incarnation had meant God revealing himself in a very qualified and impoverished way, for Barth the Incarnation is the expression (the Word) of a God who always had man, and the glorification of man, in mind. God in Christ revealed his majesty precisely in the humiliations, trials and sufferings of Christ which many theologians in the past had thought must conceal it.

The resulting shape of Barth's theological scheme gives central place to the Incarnation, Scripture, and the Church. All Christian theology turns out in the end, according to Barth, to be an aspect of Christology whether it be the doctrine of creation, or of the church, or of the sacraments.[1]

Barth may have been neo-Calvinist in his approach to the doctrine of man, emphasizing human impotence before God, but in the end his theology of man turns out to be more optimistic than, say, that of Tillich or Niebuhr. There is a warm glow about Barth's language when he writes about man as he is in Christ, re-created man. On the other hand his theology is distanced from cultural and social interests. Barth saw what he called a *diastasis,* a tension between theology and the arts where Tillich perceived the possibilities of 'correlation'.

For *Bultmann* too the 1914–18 war was a turning point. It was during this period that he was working as a New Testament scholar on the form-critical method (see pp. 37 ff.) and this proved to be determinative for his later work. He was sceptical about being able to get behind the 'kerygmatic' Christ of the gospels and sure that we do not have data for providing informed discussion about such subjects as the motivation of Christ or the self-awareness about his own mission. As well as the influence of Bultmann's scholarly investigations we need to reckon with his deep interest in the problem of communication, and his concern with the pastoral problems created by the fact that the tradition about Jesus comes down to us in a 'mythological' form. The extent of this problem was brought home to him by what he heard from army chaplains in the Second World War about their experiences in trying to preach and teach. This raised in an acute form the whole

[1] *Church Dogmatics,* I, 2, pp. 123 ff.

question of how the Christian gospel is to be communicated in the modern world. This involved a study of the status of 'mythology' in the Christian religion. Is it an essential form of human speech, or it is accidental, temporary, continually replaceable by more satisfactory translations or paraphrases into other kinds of language? Bultmann came to believe the latter and hence insisted upon the need for 'demythologizing' (see pp. 64 ff.).

Bultmann took over the language of 'existentialist' philosophy as that which is specially well equipped to express the kind of religious belief we find in the New Testament. 'Existentialist' thinking is that in which we are ourselves personally involved, the kind of thinking in which we are personally implicated. It calls for personal decision and genuine commitment. Existentialism is antipathetic to any philosophy which is merely theoretical or academic (in the bad sense). The debate started by Bultmann's transposition of New Testament belief into existentialist terms has centred on whether this emphasis on the subjective, on *my* decision and commitment here and now, is adequate to do justice to the many facets of Christianity. Is not the New Testament also concerned with certain objective facts, like the redemption wrought by Christ, which remain true irrespective of any personal decision and commitment. Sometimes after reading a lot of Bultmann one has the feeling that when the existentialist theologian says 'God' he really means 'me'. Or at least it sounds like that!

Bultmann shares the hesitations of Barth about exposing the Incarnation to the ambiguities and probabilities of historical investigation. This would make faith vulnerable to the hazards of historical criticism and Bultmann, like Barth, seems intent on finding some area for faith which is immune from that eventuality.

So the data for theology which is to determine one's starting point is not the world, nor is it the Bible in the way Barth takes it, although the New Testament plays a cardinal role in Bultmann's theology. Rather it is human existence, because this is where the whole question of faith is posed. The mythological idiom of the New Testament really relates to man in his existential predicaments, to the need for decision, and for turning from 'inauthentic' to 'authentic' existence.

When we turn to *Paul Tillich* we find a theologian who is very much closer than Barth or Bultmann to the liberal tradition and to principles of liberal investigation. Tillich's whole approach to theology is based on the assumption that man has a natural ability to apprehend truth and that there is in man 'a depth of reason'. He starts from anthropology, examining the implications of the questions which are set by human existence.

Tillich agreed with Barth that theology is 'kerygmatic' but he insisted that it is also 'apologetic'. He kept a place for 'natural theology'. If theology is treated as only 'kerygmatic' Tillich believed, and I think rightly, that it then becomes irrelevant outside the domestic circle of believers, and is only useful for 'revivalism', as he put it.

Tillich departed radically from Bultmann on the question of myth and symbol. 'Demythologizing' for Tillich was an impossible enterprise because the myth is by its very nature irreplaceable and untranslatable, and cannot be transposed into a paraphrase without serious distortion or reduction. 'Myth' is a significant pattern of symbols organized into a narrative story which has the peculiar power, whenever it is receptively read or heard of bringing with it a clearer perception and deeper understanding of some feature of human experience which can not be evoked or expressed in any other way. Tillich believed that myth was therefore fundamentally irreplaceable. Bultmann on the other hand does not see myth existing in its own permanent right, but rather as a temporary way of putting things in a certain culture, which may now be seen perhaps as striking and picturesque, but not a necessary form of human speech.

Tillich was outstanding among the group represented in this series, and indeed in the twentieth century generally, for the attention he gave to analysing the relation between theology and culture. On this issue he was far removed from Barth and closer to a thinker like Niebuhr.

Reinhold Niebuhr's work can also be seen as a reaction against the preceding liberal theology. He is specially critical of the tendencies in nineteenth-century theology to equate the 'kingdom of God' with social betterment or progress. His theological endeavour could be described as an essay in 'prophetic realism'. He sought, that is to say, to relate biblical insights into the meaning of history and God's judgement on and in it to the political and social situation of his day. His aim was 'realism' in the sense that he had a deep suspicion of what one American writer has called 'the men of the infinite', that is the idealists, the romantics, the men of abstract generalization. Niebuhr preferred the company of 'the men of the finite', those with a careful eye for data, evidence, facts. A good example of this 'prophetic realism' is to be found in the essay 'The ultimate trust' in *Beyond Tragedy*.

Like Tillich, but unlike Barth, Niebuhr starts from the human situation. Here again one finds his work a marked contrast to nineteenth-century liberalism in the way he expounds afresh the doctrines of the 'fall of man' and 'original sin', and the place he gives to eschatology. The basic form of sin for Niebuhr is not finitude or imperfection but the anxiety about them which human freedom makes possible and which expresses itself in pride and envy.

Niebuhr takes up from liberal theology the results of biblical criticism, especially as it affects biblical history. 'Fundamentalist' approaches to the Bible blurred the distinction between different literary forms, and, most disastrously, between symbolic language and language of historical fact.

The theology of *Bonhoeffer*, fragmentary though it be, is of the greatest importance in showing a man struggling to free himself from various traditions in his early training, notably the influence of Karl Barth, and re-cast the whole structure of theology to face a new situation. Bonhoeffer came to believe that the theology of Barth and Bultmann had seriously neglected the social and political problems of the world. In this respect he found the theology of Niebuhr, which he came to know well as a result of his visits to America, very much more congenial.

Bonhoeffer was very much concerned with the significance of Christ, and especially the place of the historical Christ in Christian belief. His theology is, in one respect, an attempt to reconstruct a Christocentric theology and ethics just as thoroughgoing in its Christocentricity as Barth's. He does not, however, isolate the place and role of the Bible in the manner of Barth nor does he put the whole stress on inwardness in the existentialist fashion of Bultmann and Tillich.

4

The theologians represented in this series are already established figures on the twentieth-century theological scene, and their writings have by now attained the status of 'classics'. What developments have there been among a younger genera- of theologians? Recently a number of new movements have come into vogue which could be given the labels: 'The new theology', 'Secular Christianity' and 'The death of God theology'. There is space here only for a brief word about each of these developments.

One of the most astonishing phenomena in recent years has been the popular success of Dr John A. T. Robinson's *Honest to God*, first published in 1963, which has now sold well over one million copies, as well as being translated into a great number of foreign languages. The extraordinary circulation of this book is strange because it was not written for a popular audience, it contains long extracts from Tillich, Bultmann and Bonhoeffer which make severe demands on the general reader, and it could not be described as a piece of creative or lucid theological writing. The author would be the first to say that he was not attempting a new theology but to promote a discussion of the three thinkers just mentioned who had hitherto, especially in this country, been known only by academics and professional theologians. It was perhaps the tone of voice of this book rather than its contents which gave it such popular appeal particularly since the author was a bishop, with all that the image of such a person still implies in this country. The picture which the book suggested of a bishop not pontificating theological certainties in dogmatizing fashion, but exploring in a very tentative way and voicing his own doubts and un- certainties, struck a new note for many people. *Honest to God* appeared to be the manifesto of a movement of liberation, and to express the feeling that belief was a continuous dialogue with doubt within each person, and not an unchangeable certainty over against the unbelief of others.

Many critics have pointed out the obscurities and confusions in Dr Robinson's book. One of these is significant and worth pausing over. This is the question of the place and function of metaphor in religious language which he brings up in the first chapter on the God 'up there or out there'. He expresses his irritation with this kind of language but without making it at all clear what he takes a phrase like 'God is up there' to mean. If he is arguing that God is not 'up there' in the sense that God is not an entity that one could theoretically examine in, say, the course of space exploration, this is an assertion not to be found in traditional Christian theology. There is, however, a sense in which it is most true to say that God is 'up there' or 'out there' and that is that 'God' is not simply another word for human life or experience at its most profound or intense. It is not clear, on this basic issue, which of the two uses the bishop has in mind.

This is a very significant area of confusion and it pinpoints what is a real situation of crisis in contemporary theology. This is 'the crisis of metaphor', and it bears on the discussions about 'myth' and symbolism to be found in a number of the extracts given in this series. Man as a finite being is bound to be a metaphor-making animal so long as he experiences intimations of realities outside or beyond what can be measured scientifically. This means, at the least, so long as he remains capable of aesthetic, moral, and mystical experience. The fact, for instance, that to indicate these experiences he uses the spatial language of a 'three-decker' universe ('up there', 'down there') is not the 'scandal' that Bultmann and Dr Robinson take it to be. This is a serious misplacing of what is the real 'stumbling-block' for twentieth-century man as far as Christian language is concerned. In fact the 'three-decker' universe is not a bad image to use in any talk about values and religious beliefs, at least for finite man in a space-time universe which is likely to be the condition of most of mankind in the foreseeable future. For spaceless man no doubt another image would be necessary, but until it is demonstrated that spacelessness is to be the permanent human state to try and dispense with spatial or temporal metaphor or even to be coy about its use is not a sign of maturity or progress. It indicates an inhuman and senseless attempt to try and jump out of our

finite skin. The momentum of the human mind, as the poet
Wallace Stevens put it, is towards abstraction. Part of the
appeal of a 'demythologized' version of Christianity, suggested
by Bultmann and others, and commended by Dr Robinson, is
that it takes one away from the trying particularities of the
concrete. But 'concretization', to use Bonhoeffer's term, is a
necessary undertaking for the Christian religion as long as it is
firmly rooted in an historical and particular Incarnation. It is
this feature of the Christian religion which indicates where the
real 'stumbling-block' for modern man has to be placed. This
is precisely where St Paul put it, in the enigmatical ambiguity
of a Christ who is so identified with the human scene as to be,
seemingly, indistinguishable from it, except to the eyes of faith.

It would be generally true to say that all the theologians
represented in this series took a view about the task of philosophy which has now become very unfashionable in Britain.
They believed the job of the philosopher was to build up a
world-view, a 'metaphysics'. Both Barth and Tillich shared this
view. Barth suspected that the very 'world-view' inherent in
philosophy would blur the distinctiveness of Christianity. Bultmann believed that 'existentialism' provided a coherent 'metaphysics' of human existence. Niebuhr and the earlier Bonhoeffer
approached philosophy in the same way.

It is the special interest of Paul van Buren's *The Secular
Meaning of the Gospel* (1963) that it discusses the relation
between Christian theology and the type of linguistic or
analytical philosophy which has developed in Britain and the
United States. For philosophers like Ludwig Wittgenstein,
G. E. Moore and A. J. Ayer the task of the philosopher is not
to construct a 'world-view', but to analyse and classify
language. The philosopher studies how language works and the
meanings which we attach to statements. He seeks to establish
ways of verifying the truth of the various assertions we make.

In the first wave of linguistic analysis popularized by A. J.
Ayer's *Language, Truth and Logic* (1936) it was asserted that
the only kind of language which had meaning was that which
was scientifically verifiable. All other types of language, poetry,
for example, or moral exhortation or religion, were said to be
meaningless because they were not susceptible to this kind of
verification. Philosophical linguistic analysis has modified this

position in recent years, and the concern now is how to classify the uses of language and to discuss the types of meaning appropriate to each in relation to the contexts in which they are used.

Paul van Buren seeks to relate the exposition of Christian theology to this kind of linguistic philosophical analysis. Also he has in mind the wish expressed by Bonhoeffer that one ought to be seeking for a 'non-religious interpretation' of biblical and theological concepts. van Buren's book has been nicknamed 'The case of the disappearing gospel'. Certainly in the process of re-stating Christianity in 'non-religious' language he so dissolves traditional Christian theology that it is difficult to see what if anything a believer of former times would recognize in it as familiar.

In *The Secular Meaning of the Gospel* van Buren contended that there is a residual Christianity, even when one has abandoned the idea that any meaning can be attached to 'God' or the 'transcendent'. This remainder he turns into a kind of moral heroism. Christ becomes for all men a model, *the* paradigm, of 'openness' and freedom. The significance of Christ is that he has shown himself, and continues to show himself, to be a potent example of these qualities.

The most recent phase of theology has been called the 'death of God' movement. This is the title of a book by Gabriel Vahanian, and it has been used to describe the work not only of Vahanian but of Thomas Altizer (*The Gospel of Christian Atheism*) and William Hamilton, *The Essence of Christianity*.

If one complained about confusion in *Honest to God* this complaint would have to be brought even more sharply against some of these theologians, especially Altizer, whose work is irritatingly rhapsodic just at the points where clarity of expression is most required. It is not at all easy to be sure of what exactly is being said. In one way Altizer seems to be saying that Nietzsche's cry, 'God is dead', still needs repeating, particularly since as far as modern man in a technological society is concerned belief in God as a transcendent reality upon whom mankind depends has no meaning, and is hopelessly irrelevant. Man must now look to his own resources as he prepares to take charge of his own evolution.

Another side of Altizer seems to be saying, again in a very

confused way, that Christians have been reluctant to come to
realistic terms with the Incarnation, particularly with its
corollary that Christ really died the death. This is a useful
point because it is true that Christians have traditionally not
only denied that Christ was born in the way that we are, but
there remained for a long time in Christian theology, especially
in the Greek church, the belief that Christ's human flesh was
not mortal flesh as ours is.

Altizer wishes to press the reality of the *kenosis* or self-
giving in Incarnation so that one can say with Charles Péguy,
'God too has faced death'. But Altizer seems to take *kenosis*
to mean a literal self-annihilation. He speaks of the death of
God as 'an historical event'. If these words mean anything
Altizer is saying that in the Incarnation God, as it were, com-
mitted suicide. The death of God in Christ has freed us to
become our own Christs, the result of the Incarnation being
that God has diffused himself in the human race. This sounds
like a new version of pantheism.

What is specially interesting in the 'death of God' theologians
is the place which they are still willing to accord to Christ. In
spite of form-criticism and the wave of scepticism which it
produced both Altizer and Hamilton seem to believe that there
is sufficiently reliable information available about Jesus to
warrant our thinking again about the ideal of the 'imitation
of Christ'. This is interpreted along very different lines from
Bonhoeffer's presentation of the *imitatio Christi*. It reminds
one of what Kierkegaard called 'admiration of Christ', a
herioc endeavour to reproduce his 'openness' and 'freedom'
by sheer effort of will.

5

It is hazardous to suggest what is likely to be the prospect for
theology in the rest of this century. However, it seems to me
that four areas will provide material for special clarification:
(1) There is first what I have called the 'crisis of metaphor'
in modern theology. Theology and religious language stand or
fall by metaphor and all that it implies about human life and
human perception. The impulse to metaphor, to speak of one

thing in terms of another, prompts the question whether the relation between appearance and reality may not be of the kind which religious belief suggests. The surrender of metaphor means the end of religion and, significantly, the death of what we have come to regard as distinctively human feelings. The French 'anti-novelist' Alain Robbe-Grillet is perfectly right to detect an important link between metaphor and religion. Robbe-Grillet wishes to get rid of metaphor because it implies some hidden relationship between man and the universe, and this takes us half-way to religion. Indeed, there is a 'crisis of metaphor' in modern literature as well as in modern theology. Bultmann can speak disparagingly of 'mere metaphors' and advocates 'demythologization' because myth, metaphor and symbol can be taken in a crude literal way, or can become obsolete. These are certainly hazards in the human situation, which often necessitate a drastic process of unlearning. But a worse fate, a greater hurt to the soul is to attempt to bring about a state of affairs where such hazards are no longer possible. It is damaging either to identify metaphor and actuality or to romanticize pantheistically (in a way that alarms Robbe-Grillet), but it is worse to believe that as individuals and as a generation we have gone beyond the need for metaphor. At stake, therefore, in the present 'crisis of metaphor' in literature and religion is nothing less than the humanization or dehumanization of man.

(2) There needs to be very much more exploration of what Tillich called 'correlation' between religion and the arts. Christians have lived too long with the assumption that while art may have aesthetic or pedagogical value, it is no serious avenue to truth. Art has been regarded as useful for those who cannot read, and need pictures, but not for the literate who having mastered discursive reasoning and the manipulation of abstractions have no need of the image. Art has therefore been taken by many theologians to be inferior to philosophy, and on the whole Christian theologians have preferred to cultivate relations with philosophers rather than artists. This is, however, to beg the question whether art is a way of knowing which is as truth-bearing, in its way, as philosophical or scientific method. Christians have surrendered with amazing ease to the notion that the image is a lesser form of truth than the con-

cept, as if image and concept were simply alternative ways of saying the same thing, except that the image helps those who have more imagination than logic. It is arguable that the Christian religion would have gained as much (perhaps more) from association with art as it has from philosophy, not only for general apologetic reasons, but for intellectual arguments with what Schleiermacher called its 'cultural despisers'.

(3) Thirdly, there is the continuing work of interpreting afresh the significance of Christ and in the immediate future this will have to include a thorough exploration of what it means to talk about the uniqueness of Christ and his finality.

In spite of the central place which it occupies in the structure of their beliefs, it has proved persistently difficult for Christians to take the Incarnation with full realism and to follow through its implications in a rigorously realistic way. It took Christians a very long time indeed to accept the belief that the Incarnation meant taking a human biology exactly like ours. What a struggle there was in the early Church to get accepted the belief that Christ really died the death in the way that we do! The history of the iconography of the crucifixion in art shows that it took nearly five centuries before a body of Christ appeared on the cross, and then it is very much a live Christ who, eyes open, stands on the cross as a royal warrior looking through the scene. It took the Christian Church nearly ten centuries before a really dead body of Christ appeared on the cross, and even then it was not a death in suffering and agony. It is another century and a half before a bleeding, suffering emaciated Christ with a crown of thorns appears in the representation of the crucifixion. This is a long time, but it has taken Christians even longer to come anywhere near accepting that the Incarnation involved taking a genuine human psychology of the kind that might mean that Christ had to find his way to religious belief in exactly the same way as everybody else, through faith, through acting on signs which, because they are ambiguous and our freedom is real, can always be 'stumbling-bocks' ('scandals' in the New Testament) that offend. Just as dangerous as a theology based on the 'God of the gaps' has been a 'Christology of the gaps', that is, a tendency to insert a capacity for full divine self-awareness on

• •

the part of the historical Jesus in some 'gap' in his psyche, or, so it has sometimes been suggested, in his subconscious!

The question of the finality of Christ suggests the fourth area in which it is likely that theology will be specially engaged in the immediate future: comparative religion, and especially comparative theology.

(4) In the contemporary world it sometimes appears that the 'ecumenical' movement of unbelief grows faster than that of belief, so that all religions are finding themselves on the same side of the fence as far as faith that human life has a transcendental significance is concerned. In this situation there needs to be more conversation between the theologies of the religions, particularly those whose history gives them a special kinship: Judaism, Christianity and Islam. If the Christian has to start thinking again about the meaning of Incarnation and the unique place which he assigns to Christ there is no more bracing company in which he could explore this question than that of the Jew and Muslim.

The present-day student of the Christian doctrines of the Trinity and the Incarnation might well begin with reflection on the familiar strictures on these doctrines that come from the Jew and the Muslim: that they violate the concept of the unity of God, and, by involving God in human history in a finite way, blaspheme against the majesty of God. The Christian will want to have as rich a doctrine that God is one as the Jew or the Muslim, and that God is known in historical event, and perhaps this is now more likely to be attained by going to school theologically with these two religions. Further the three religions of Judaism, Christianity and Islam have much to give each other in working out afresh for our own day the meaning of what it is to be human. Bishop Kenneth Cragg has shown how profound a realization of the nature of man comes from relating the Jewish/Christian concept of man made in the 'image of God' to the Muslim concept of man as God's 'caliph'.[1]

Much needs to be unlearned and relearned in this field. Judaism, Islam and Buddhism have suffered from misleading propagandist slogans in the past like 'Jewish legalism', 'Islam

[1] Kenneth Cragg, *The Privilege of Man*, London, 1968.

2—MTS-2 * *

is the most materialistic and least religious of the religions',
'Buddhism is insensitive to suffering or social justice'. These
are Christian caricatures of the truth, and there is now a fresh
chance, especially in those western countries which are now
multi-religious, to rectify this distortion by mutual understanding in co-operative study.

BIOGRAPHICAL INTRODUCTION

There is an astonishing contrast between the uneventful life of Bultmann and the dramatic and controversial role which he has played in biblical studies and Christian theology in the first half of the twentieth century. He was born in 1884 in Wiefelstede which was then part of the Grand Duchy of Oldenburg in north-west Germany. He came from clerical stock, both sides of the family having produced pastors. He had a country upbringing and speaks of his schooldays as a time of happiness. Outside his religious interests he read a good deal of German and Greek literature, and he was keen on music concerts and the theatre.

He decided to study theology at the University and was a student at Tübingen, Berlin and Marburg. He began his academic career at Marburg when he was appointed to a lectureship.

He has known the scars of his generation. He had one brother killed in the First World War, and another in a Nazi concentration camp in the Second World War.

In 1916 he was appointed assistant professor at Breslau, where Bonhoeffer was born, and in 1920 became full professor at Giessen. The following year he returned as professor to his old university of Marburg in which he remained until his retirement in 1951.

He took up a pronounced anti-Nazi attitude but was not involved in underground activity in the way Bonhoeffer was.

Since his retirement he has lectured in the United States and elsewhere.

SELECTIONS

1 FORM-CRITICISM

[The work of the later Bultmann, especially his programme of 'demythologizing', can only be understood in the light of his earlier researches as a New Testament critic. He was one of the 'founding-fathers' of New Testament 'form-criticism' and these extracts give some illustration of its methods.

Bultmann discusses first the comparative literary study of the gospels. This showed that Mark was the first of the New Testament gospels to achieve written form, and that it had been used (with adaptations) as one of their sources by the authors of *St Matthew* and *St Luke*. Following this discovery, Mark's gospel was used to try and reconstruct the historical mission of Jesus and, in particular, the development of his 'messianic self-consciousness'. The results of this effort were however inconclusive.

Bultmann then turns to a description of form-criticism, pointing out first the amplifications and modifications which any tradition undergoes as it is handed on by word of mouth. Form-criticism tries to isolate and analyse characteristic units of the tradition about Christ, like, for example, 'miracle-stories' and 'sayings-stories' (apothegms), and to place them in the history of the formation of the gospels.]

(a) The Literary study of the Gospels

The second feature of contemporary Gospel research is the new literary-historical method of approach which has come to be known as Form-criticism. As we have noted, research had already arrived at the result that the Gospel of Mark was the oldest of the three Synoptics, and that by its side was to be found the collection of Sayings as another old source. It was assumed in the generation of such experts as H. J. Holtzmann, A. Julicher, and J. Weiss that one could make out from Mark and Q (the Sayings-document) the course of the life of Jesus and the content of his preaching with relative certainty. The inner development of the life of Jesus was inferred from the development of his Messianic consciousness: that is, from his steadily advancing claim to Messiahship, of which he was not entirely certain at the beginning and accordingly kept secret, and which he publicly acknowledged only at the end of his life; which consciousness as it gradually ripened in himself he permitted gradually to ripen likewise in his disciples. The outward development of his life, on the other hand, was characterized by an initial success and then by a gradual desertion on the part of the people, whose hopes he had disappointed, and most of all by the opposition of the scribes and Pharisees. The chief content of the preaching of Jesus was his message of the Kingdom of God, which was neither a purely spiritual state nor a society of the pious realizing itself historically in the midst of this world, but was the heavenly Kingdom expected to come miraculously and catastrophically in the immediate future. These scholars scarcely recognized the problem, viz., how the moral demands of Jesus were related to this 'eschatological' message—the former receiving expression in many of his sayings (e.g., Matt. v. 20–45; vi. 1–34) and in the controversies with the scribes, and containing practically no traces of the eschatological expectation.

On the other hand, W. Wrede had already demonstrated in his book *The Messianic Secret in the Gospels* (*Das Messiasgeheimnis in den Evangelien*, 1901), undoubtedly the most important work in the field of gospel research in the generation now past, that although Mark is indeed the oldest gospel, its narrative cannot be accepted as an exact account of the history of Jesus; that Mark is really dominated by the theology of the Church and by a dogmatic conception of Christ; and that he arranged and revised the old traditional material out of which his gospel is composed in accordance with his own ideas, so that one cannot make out from his narrative either the development of the Messianic consciousness and claim of Jesus or the course of his activity, nor the reasons for his failure and death. Wellhausen[1] in his *Commentaries on the Gospels* (1905 and following) reinforced and demonstrated essentially the same conclusion : in each of the gospels one must distinguish between the old tradition and the redactional

[1] Julius Wellhausen (1844–1918), distinguished German biblical scholar. (Ed.)

contribution of the evangelists; the former consists essentially in single brief units; the latter not only altered many of the details but first gave its continuity to the whole, thus creating the artificial effect of a historical development. Especially important is Wellhausen's demonstration that the Sayings-document, like Mark, has been influenced by the theology of the primitive Church : it grew out of the primitive community and is steeped in its views and interests, and therefore gives us no infallible reflection of the preaching of Jesus.

The result of these works was at once a widespread but perfectly futile discussion of the Messianic consciousness of Jesus. To what extent had Jesus looked upon himself as Messiah in the Jewish sense, to what extent did he transform the Jewish Messianic conception? Did he look upon himself as Messiah from the very beginning—say from the time of his baptism—or did his Messianic consciousness grow gradually, first developing, perhaps, towards the end of his ministry? Was the Messianic consciousness for him a matter of pride and of consolation in the midst of opposition, or was it a burden hard to bear? Was it essential or was it a relatively indifferent form of his sense of vocation? These were the typical questions, and all of these tantalizing possibilities were investigated by individual scholars and variously affirmed and denied; one can scarcely gain a stronger impression of the uncertainty of our knowledge concerning the person of Jesus than by putting together what the various investigators of the Messianic consciousness of Jesus have thought. It is noteworthy that little attention has been given to the outward course of the life of Jesus and the grounds of his condemnation. The assurance with which formerly it was assumed that the ministry of Jesus was limited to one year has indeed weakened since it has come to be recognized that the outline of Mark is not historical. But what were the actual external factors determining his fate, and what it was that led him to the cross—these questions are scarcely asked, as if it were self-evident that the enmity of the scribes and Pharisees compassed his death. The problem, how the eschatological and the ethical teaching of Jesus are related one to the other, has come at last to be recognized. It is in truth far from easy to say how an eschatological prophet who sees the end of the world approaching, who senses the arrival of the Kingdom of God, and accordingly pronounces blessed those of his contemporaries who are prepared for it (Matt. 13 : 16–17; 5 : 3–9; 11 : 5–6 etc.)—to say how such a person could argue over questions of the Law and turn off epigrammatic proverbs like a Jewish rabbi (since to practically all the moral directions of Jesus there are parallel and related words of Jewish rabbis), in words which contain simply no hint of eschatological tension (e.g., Matt. 6 : 19–21, 25–34; 7 : 1, 2, 7; 10 : 29; Luke 14 : 7–11; Mark 2 : 27; 4 : 21). Wellhausen looked upon the ethical teaching as the genuine historical nucleus, and believed that the eschatological sayings were for the most part of the products of the primitive Christian community, which after Jesus' death was strongly influenced by the Messianic expectations. Others, like J. Weiss and A. Schweitzer, held, contrariwise, the eschatological preaching to be the characteristic message of the historical Jesus, and either ignored the moral directions or explained them as 'interim ethic', that is, as requirements which lacked general validity but which held good for this last brief space of time which was to precede the end.

(b) *The Method of Form-criticism*

Form-criticism begins with the observation that, especially in primitive literature, literary expression (oral or written) makes use of more or less fixed forms, which have their own laws of style. In the Old Testament we have long been accustomed to recognize this feature and to apply the form-historical method. The forms of psalm, prayer, prophetic address, fable, story, and historical narrative have been recognized and their stylistic laws have been described. Is it possible to identify similar literary forms in the Synoptic tradition? If this be the case, one must recognize and reckon with the fact that the tradition possesses a certain solidarity, since the form would naturally oppose itself to any serious alterations. On the other hand, it will be possible to determine in the individual sections whether the appropriate form was purely expressed or somewhat revised, and so one should be able to determine the age of the section. This would be the more true if it were possible to recognize not only the appropriate laws of style of a specified literary form but also the laws by which the further development of material takes place, i.e., a certain orderliness in change by which a body of tradition is always controlled in its growth. There are various means available to this end. The first is this, that we may accurately observe how the Marcan material is altered and revised by Matthew and Luke, and how Matthew and Luke have presumably edited the text of Q (the Sayings-document). If we are able to deduce a certain regularity in this procedure, then we may certainly assume that the same laws held good even earlier, and we may draw conclusions as to the state of the tradition prior to Mark and Q. It is clear that this is a very difficult process and one to be pursued with great caution. One may, however, test his skill by studying the manner in which the evangelical material was handed down in the later Church, especially in the apocryphal gospels, and likewise the general laws governing popular narrative and tradition, such as stories and anecdotes. In order, however, to identify the peculiar stylistic laws governing the forms of the Synoptic tradition, we must remind ourselves that certain forms were found close at hand in the environment of the early Christian community, and offered themselves for purposes of tradition. Similar sayings and brief narratives were handed down in Jewish literature, and their forms show remarkable similarity to those of the evangelical material.

(c) *The Laws Governing Popular Narrative and Tradition*

The laws governing the formulation of popular narrative and tradition may be studied in detail in the material which the Synoptists hand down. The first thing we observe is that the narrators do not give us long unified accounts but rather small single pictures, individual scenes narrated with the utmost simplicity. These always occupy but a brief space of time; apart from the Passion Narrative no event or proceeding is narrated which covered more than two days. As a rule only two speaking characters appear in these scenes, or at most three; involved proceedings are beyond the powers of the simple story teller. Where groups or crowds are present, they are treated as a unity. As such narratives pass from mouth to mouth, or when one writer takes them over from another, their fundamental character remains the same, but the details are subject to the control of fancy and are usually made more explicit and definite. So, for example, Mark 9 : 17 relates that the father brought his demoniac son to Jesus; in Luke's version is added the statement that he was an only son (9 : 38). The palsied hand which Jesus healed (Mark 3 : 1) is described by Luke as the right hand (6 : 6). The ear of the high priest's servant which was struck off in Gethsemane (Mark 14 : 47) was according to Luke 22 : 50 the right ear. One may observe in the account of this scene which appears in the Gospel of John another important law at work: though the Synoptists do not name either the servant or the disciple who struck him, John gives the names, Malchus and Peter.

In the apocryphal tradition the process may be followed still further since here legend creates the names of hitherto un-named persons; for example, those of the three Wise Men from the East, the woman with an issue of blood, the crucified robbers, the officer on guard at Jesus' tomb, and so on. How-ever, one may see such supplying of names already at work in the Synoptics. The disciples who are sent to prepare for the Last Supper are unnamed in Mark (14 : 13); in Luke their names are given, Peter and John (22 : 8). Instead of the disciples as in Mark 7 : 17, it is Peter who asks the question of Jesus in Matthew 15 : 15. The name of the ruler of the synagogue, whose daughter Jesus raised from death, is given as Jairus in Luke 8 : 41; in Mark there is a whole series of manuscripts in which the name is omitted, and it is not at all unlikely that in the others it was added to complete the text. For this reason one must be a little sceptical even of the names given in Mark (e.g., 10 : 28, 46; 11 : 21).

Still another example of the way in which fancy has elabo-rated the older material is the account of the robbers crucified with Jesus (Luke 23 : 39–43) : Mark knows nothing of this but says simply that the two men crucified with Jesus mocked him (15 : 32).

Another characteristic trait is that the narrator prefers to give in direct discourse what his source gave indirectly. For example, Mark 8 : 32 states that when Jesus announced his coming Passion, Peter upbraided him; Matthew 16 : 22 reports him as saying, 'Be it far from Thee, Lord!' Instead of the narrative of Mark 14: 1, 'After two days was the feast of the Passover and of unleavened bread', Matthew 26: 1 f. reads, 'And it came to pass when Jesus had finished all these sayings, he said unto his disciples "Ye know that after two days is the feast of the passover..."' While Mark 14 : 23 relates that when the cup was passed around at the Last Supper 'they all drank of it,' Matthew makes Jesus say 'Drink ye all of it' (26 : 27). In the account of the kiss of Judas, Mark says nothing of any words of Jesus; Matthew (26 : 50), however, and Luke (22 : 48), each introduce a saying, though each brings forward a different one—it is easy to see how imagination has elaborated this scene. The last inarticulate cry of Jesus (Mark 15 : 37) becomes in Luke the saying, 'Father, into Thy Hands I commend my spirit' (23: 46).

Still another important fact deserves to be mentioned. Along with the tendency to characterize more definitely the dim figures in the tradition goes the inclination to impose a schematic idea of the course of Jesus' activity, viz., the opponents with whom Jesus engages in disputation are almost invariably scribes and Pharisees, who interrogate him with malicious intent. One may often observe or infer that the earliest tradition had to do with unspecified questioners, whom the later narrators transformed into ill-disposed scribes or Pharisees. In the original Sayings-document (Q) it was only stated that 'some of them' accused Jesus of collusion with the devil (Luke 11 : 15); according to Matthew (12 : 24) these were Pharisees, according to Mark (3 : 22) they were scribes. Similarly the demand for a sign was made originally by some of the crowd (Luke 11 : 16); in Matthew (12 : 38) and Mark (7 : II) the demand comes from the Pharisees (and scribes). It is quite characteristic that Mark has retained in its old form the story of the question concerning the greatest commandment, in accordance with which the inquirer is entirely honest, and in the end is praised by Jesus as not far from the Kingdom of God (12 : 28–34). In Matthew this word of praise has fallen away, and the questioner appears from the outset as crafty and hypocritical (22 : 34–40; cf. Luke 10 : 25). Of course, many a polemic word of Jesus addressed to the scribes and Pharisees may be entirely historical (Mark 12 : 38–40; and most of Matt. 23 : 1–31), but the schematic representation according to which the Pharisees and scribes are from the outset the sworn enemies of Jesus is certainly unhistorical.

(d) Two types of traditional material

(i) Miracle stories

It may further be demonstrated that the evangelical material is set forth in the forms of distinct literary types. It is self-evident that the laws of style governing a literary type are more or less elastic; at the same time each type has its own definite characteristics which may be observed in every example of the type, even though these characteristics are not all present in any one example.

This may be seen for example in the miracle stories. Professor O. Weinreich has gathered together a body of material suitable for comparison under the title *Ancient Miracles of Healing (Antike Heilungswunder,* 1909), as have also P. Fiebig, *Jewish Miracle Narratives of the New Testament Period (Judische Wundergeschichten des neutestamentlichen Zeitalters,* 1911), and others. The lay reader may obtain an impression of such ancient miracle stories from a translation of the writing of Lucian of Samosata (second century A.D.), *The Friend of Lies* (Greek 'Philopseudes'). A comparison of the two makes it clear that the miracle stories of the gospels possess a remarkable resemblance to the Hellenistic miracle narratives; the latter accordingly throw significant light upon the problem of their origin or at least of their formulation.

The following seem to be characteristic of the style observed in the narratives of miracles. As a rule the narrative is given in three parts. First, the condition of the patient is described. Just as, for example, in Mark 9:18 we read, 'I have brought unto thee my son who hath a dumb spirit; and wheresoever he taketh him, he teareth him : and he foameth and gnasheth with his teeth and pineth away'—so Lucian tells the story (Philops. 16) of a certain 'Syrian from Palestine,' a 'wise man' who had understanding in these matters: he was known to have healed many, 'who fell down in fits, rolled their eyes, and foamed at the mouth'. Typical also is the emphasis upon the gravity of the illness (e.g., Mark 5 : 3–5) or its long duration (e.g., Mark 5 : 25 f.; 9 : 12; Luke 13 : II). Just as in the Greek stories, so Mark 5 : 26 describes the futile efforts of physicians to heal the illness, and also the scornful attitude of the people when the true healer first appeared (Mark 5 : 40). Just as here it is said that the crowd standing about the house of mourning laughed Jesus to scorn, so, for example, the inscriptions in the temple of the healing God Asclepios at Epidauros tell of a sick woman who laughed sceptically when she heard of the marvellous deeds of the God, or how the crowd ridiculed the folly of a man totally blind who hoped for divine healing.

In the second section of the story the healing itself is narrated. Often the peculiar manipulations of the healer are described, as in Mark 7 : 33; 8 : 23. In general, however, the New Testament miracle stories are extremely reserved in this respect, since they hesitate to attribute to the person of Jesus the magical traits which were often characteristic of the Hellenistic miracle worker. In Hellenistic stories we are told, for example, how an exorcist drove the spirit out of a demoniac by holding a ring to the patient's nose so that he might smell a marvellous root that has been set in it; or how another healed a person of snake-bite by placing upon the wounded foot a tiny piece of the gravestone of a virgin, to the accompaniment of an appropriate magic formula. In the gospels as a rule it is simply stated, as likewise in the Hellenistic narratives, that the wonder worker approaches the patient—perhaps coming to his bedside—lays his hand upon him or takes him by the hand and utters the healing word. It is also characteristic that these words are as a rule given in an unknown foreign tongue, like 'Talitha kumi' (Mark 5 : 41) and 'Ephphatha' (Mark 7 : 34). Where the view prevails that the patient is possessed by a demon we are told how the demon sensed the presence of his master, disputed with him, but was finally threatened and driven out, as in the genuine folk-tale contained in Mark 5 : 1–20. Finally, it may be noted as characteristic that not infrequently it is said that no one was present at the miracle proper; e.g., Mark 7 : 33; 8 : 23. We find some examples in the Old Testament; I Kings 17 : 19; II Kings 4 : 4, 33. The original implication of this is doubtless that no one may witness an act of deity, as in the story of Lot's wife (Genesis 19 : 26).

Two characteristics are found in the third section, as a rule. First of all it was naturally often pointed out that witnesses of the wonderful results of the miracles broke out in exclamations of wonder or approval. Not infrequently it is related of the person healed that he gave some clear demonstration of the fact : for example, the lame man taking up his bed and walking, as in Mark 2 : 11 f., and in a miracle story that Lucian relates. To the same effect is the statement that the restored daughter of Jairus was given something to eat (Mark 5 : 43); by this anyone could see that she was completely restored to life. Following the exorcism of the demons the demonstration often consists in some spiteful and destructive act of the departing demon, like the shattering of a pillar or the overturning of a bowl of water, or, as in Mark 5 : 13, the sudden frenzy of a herd of swine who dash over a cliff and fall into the sea.

(ii) *Apothegms*

Among the sayings of Jesus it is possible to distinguish various groups. There are those, for example, which have been handed down in association with a little scene, in which according to the tradition they were originally spoken. Dibelius calls such fragments of tradition 'paradigms', since he assumes that they served as illustrations in Christian preaching. I prefer to call them apothegms, since in their structure they are closely related to the narratives of Greek literature which have hitherto borne this name. It is characteristic that the narrated scene serves only as the framework for an important saying; the whole point lies in the saying, and the frame simply gives the situation in which the word was spoken, and its occasion. The occasion may be the question of a disciple or a scribe; and the question, in turn, may have been occasioned by some deed of Jesus such as a healing on the Sabbath, or by the conduct of the disciples who ate without first performing the ritual washing of hands. In such a classification belong the controversies of the Synoptic tradition, such as those in Mark 2 : 1–12, 23–

28; 3 : 1–6; 7 : 1–23 etc.; conversations with eager inquirers, as in Mark 10 : 17–22; 12 : 28–34; Matthew 11 : 2–19; Luke 17 : 20–21 etc.; and scenes of a biographical character, like Mark 6 : 1–6; 10 : 13–16; Luke 9 : 57–62; 11 : 27–28 etc. Such apothegms are to be found in Jewish literature as well as in Greek, but a closer consideration shows that there were characteristic differences between Jewish and Greek literature on this point. For the Jewish story, it is significant that the saying of the hero which is given in response to a question usually appears either as a counter-question or as a brief parable (or both at once). This is true of most of the apothegms of Jesus. A story of Rabban Gamaliel may serve as a Jewish example (Fiebig, *Erzählungsstil*, p. 103). A heathen philosopher once asked him why it was that God should be angered at idolatry, and he replied: 'Suppose a man calls his dog by the name of his father, and when he makes a vow uses the words, "By the life of this dog"; with whom will the father be angry, with the son or with the dog?' Another example is a dispute over the resurrection of the dead (Strack-Billerbeck, *Kommentar*, I, p. 895): 'The Emperor Hadrian said to Rabban Gamaliel, "You say that the dead will come back to life again; on the contrary they have turned to dust, and can dust come to life again?" Then Gamaliel's daughter spoke up and said to her father, "Never mind, let me answer him! In our city", she said, "there were two potters. One made his vessels out of water and the other out of clay. Which of these two deserves the greater praise?" The Emperor replied, "The one who made vessels out of water", and she said, "If God is able to create man out of moisture, how much more can he do so out of clay ! " ' This is the way the Synoptic controversies go. For example, Jesus replies (Mark 2 : 19) to the question, why his disciples do not fast, with the parabolic question, 'Do the sons of the bride-chamber (the bridegroom's companions) fast while the bridegroom is still with them?' To the invidious question whether or not he will heal on the Sabbath (Mark 3 : 4), he replies with the counter-question, 'Is it lawful to do good on the Sabbath day, or to do evil?' Similar counter-questions and parables are given in reply to the accusation of collusion with Satan in Mark 3 : 24–26 (cf. Mark 2 : 25 f.; 11 : 30; Luke 13 : 15, 14 : 5; Matthew 17 : 25). One may safely infer that these narratives have almost all been formulated in a Jewish environment and do not belong to the later Hellenistic period of development.

It is characteristic of the Greek apothegm that it is introduced with some such formula as, 'When he was asked by . . .', or 'Once when he observed how. . . .' We may give an example or two of this style. 'When asked by the Tyrant Dionysius why it was that philosophers visited the rich rather than the rich the philosophers, Aristippus replied: "The philosophers realize what they lack, but the rich do not".' 'Anaxagoras of Klazomenai, when he was asked why we are here, replied, " To behold the works of nature".' 'Once when Demonax saw two philosophers engaged in a thorougly discreditable argument, in which one of them asked foolish questions, and the other replied with irrelevancies, he said, "My friends, do you not realize that one of you is milking a ram and the other is holding up a sieve?" ' 'As Diogenes once saw a child drinking out of its hands, he threw away the cup that he had in his wallet and said, "A child has exceeded me in doing without things".' The passage in Luke 17:20-21 is formulated in this manner: 'And when he was demanded of the Pharisees, when the Kingdom of God should come, he answered them and said, "The Kingdom of God cometh not with observation: neither shall they say, Lo here! or lo there! for, behold, the Kingdom of God is [at once] among you".' Similar to this is the narrative contained in one manuscript of Luke 6:5: 'On the same day when he saw a man working on the Sabbath he said to him. "Man, if you know what you are doing you are happy! but if you do not know, then you are accursed and a breaker of the law." ' It may accordingly be concluded that these two accounts were first formulated in the Hellenistic church. However, it is not only possible but really probable that in Luke 17:20-21 only the framework, the scene, is a later creation and that the saying of Jesus is derived from the older tradition. One must therefore distinguish carefully between those apothegms in which the framework and the saying are so closely related that one cannot be told without the other (e.g., Mark 2:18-19; 3:1-5; Luke 12:13-14—'And one of the company said unto him, "Master speak to my brother, that he divide the inheritance with me", but he said unto him, "Man, who made me a judge or a divider over you?" '), and others, in which the framework and the saying are only loosely connected. Among the latter it is often only the saying of Jesus which is original and the frame has been supplied later; e.g., Mark 7:1–23; 10:2–12. Especially significant is Mark 2:15–17, Jesus' saying reads, 'They that are whole have no need of the physician but they that are sick; I come not to call the righteous but sinners'; the setting in vv. 15 f. has been artistically supplied later. This is indicated by the wholly unmotivated, and literally impossible, appearance of the Pharisaic scribes at a dinner attended by publicans, and further by the remarkable fact that it is the disciples who are questioned and Jesus who replies—and the same is true of other sayings in the series. The effort was made to introduce the traditional words of Jesus as completely as possible into scenes in his life, and in this case the setting of a meal seemed to be the most appropriate situation, since fellowship at table easily symbolized fellowship in general. One may further observe in other cases that unattached sayings of Jesus have been introduced into older apothegms or fastened on to them; examples of the former are found in Matthew 12:11 f.; Luke xiv. 5; of the latter in Mark 2:27 f.; 7:9–23; 10:23–27.

Striking also is a further observation that may be made: in Mark 2:18–19, 23–26; 7:1–8, it is related that the disciples did not fast, that they rubbed out kernels of grain on the Sabbath, and that they did not observe the ritual washing before meals. How are we to explain the fact that all these things are told of the disciples and not of Jesus himself, and that Jesus is called upon to defend their conduct rather than his own? It is impossible to assume that in all these instances his own conduct was correct; for the disciples can have learned their free attitude only from him! Nor may one suppose that the opponents hesitated to attack him directly; since in other cases, e.g., with reference to the healings on the Sabbath, they had no such hesitation.

Apparently the situation is to be understood only as follows: these traditions first arose in the Christian community and are to be explained by its situation. The 'disciples', i.e., the primitive Christian Church, have broken with the old customs in this matter, and they are defending themselves against criticism by means of the stories, through which they make their appeal to a saying of Jesus. It is certainly possible that the saying of Jesus enshrined in such a setting is old and authentic, as, for example, probably Mark 2:19. In the other cases it is less probable, since here argumentative use is made of sentences from the Old Testament, and since most of the words of Jesus which cite the Old Testament are suspected of originating in the theological debates of the primitive community. Just as the Messiah was defended by an appeal to Old Testament passages, so likewise an effort was made to found Christian practice upon a similar appeal.

Those apothegms which are of a biographical character are likewise for the most part creations of the community, since they give expression to what Christians had experienced of their Master or what he had experienced at the hands of his people. It is accordingly clear that the calling of the disciples in Mark 1:16–20 reflects no historical situation; the story completely lacks motivation and psychological probability. The scene sets forth symbolically and picturesquely the common experience of the disciples as they were raised by Jesus' wonderful power out of their previous spheres of life. It is in this way that we must also explain Mark 3:31–35 (Jesus' true relatives); 12:41–44 (the widow's mite); Luke 9:57–62 (various followers); 10:38–42 (Mary and Martha). Even the scene in Nazareth (Mark 6:1–6) may perhaps not reflect a particular historical event, but is rather a symbolical picture, setting forth the attitude of the people as a whole to the preaching of Jesus. As evidence for this may be cited the saying of Jesus found in one of the papyri:

'No prophet is welcome in his own home town;

And no physician can cure those who know him well.'

It may be that the scene in Mark has been created out of this saying.

(e) Our Knowledge of the Historical Jesus

What then is the final solution of the three involved problems described above: the Messianic consciousness of Jesus, the outward course of his life (and especially the grounds of his condemnation), and the relation between his eschatological and his ethical message?

Regarding the origin and development of his Messianic consciousness, we are, generally speaking, unable to say anything definite. Indeed, it must remain questionable whether Jesus regarded himself as Messiah at all, and did not rather first become Messiah in the faith of the community. The majority of scholars remain convinced of the first alternative. To me it appears rather that the second is the necessary consequence of the analysis of his words. At any rate, one may clearly see that Jesus did not come forward with the claims which from the Jewish point of view the Messianic title involved, but rather that his ministry was rightly characterized when it was said he was a prophet. Nevertheless, the movement which he inaugurated among the Jewish people may, and really must, be described as a Messianic movement, since it was carried on with the conviction that the Messianic prophecies were about to be fulfilled, that the Kingdom of God was about to appear, and that the signs of its arrival were to be seen in the mighty works of Jesus, chiefly in the banishment of the evil spirits. To those who stood outside it, this movement must have appeared like any of the other Messianic movements which in those decades convulsed the Jewish people and finally led to the war with Rome and the destruction of Jerusalem. The Roman procurators suppressed such movements with blood, and Jesus fell a victim to the intervention of the procurator Pilate. As he came up to Jerusalem with his followers his arrival was viewed by the procurator as politically dangerous. Whatever part the Jewish authorities took therein cannot now be made out, since the Passion Narrative is too thickly overgrown with legend. For the later Christians the real enemies were the Jews; since they were found to be their standing enemies and accusers, in the work of the Christian mission (note the representation in the Book of Acts), they were also made responsible for the death of Jesus. It is, of course, possible that the Jewish court in Jerusalem, in order to demonstrate its own political innocence, had some part in the tragedy; but at all events we are not entitled to assume that Jesus' ethical teaching so roused the Pharisees and scribes against him that he finally fell victim

to their enmity. That the steady opposition of the Pharisees
and scribes rests upon the artificial and schematic conception
of later Christians has already been shown.

The most important question is that concerning the content
of Jesus' preaching. The investigation has shown that both the
eschatological and the ethical teaching of Jesus belong equally
to the oldest stratum of the tradition, so that one can hardly
call either one of them secondary. Nor can we view the ethical
precepts of Jesus as 'interim-ethic'[1] for his demands have an
absolute character, and are by no means influenced in their
formulation by the thought that the end of the world is near
at hand. Consequently, both sides of the message of Jesus, the
eschatological and the ethical, must be conceived as belonging
together. Did Jesus preach the new ethic simply as a condition
of entrance into the Kingdom of God? In form this is certainly
true again and again; and yet this would be no real union of
the two elements, but only a superficial and external relation,
which, precisely in view of the earnestness of his moral
demands, would be hard to conceive. Or is the announcement
of the coming Reign of God only the mythological or
symbolical form, in which he set forth his general faith in God
as the Judge and Rewarder? One can scarcely combine this
with the moral earnestness of his prophetic mission.

We must probably conclude that in the eschatological as in
the ethical teaching of Jesus the same fundamental view of
God and of man is presupposed. The eschatological expectation
arose out of the conviction that God is the final Reality, before
whom everything earthly fades away, and before whom man
in his unworthiness and worthlessness sinks to nothing. Only
the future, which is God's, can bring salvation to man; and this
future still faces man, in the present, and requires of him the
decision for the world or for God. This is exactly the sense
that Jesus' moral demands held. Jesus sets forth neither an
individual nor a social ethics; that is, he measured the deeds
of men neither according to an ideal conception of human
personality nor of human society, but he taught men that the
present instant is the moment of decision, in which it is

[1] An ethic not for all time but only for the interval between Jesus's
own time and the 'End' which he believed to be imminent. The phrase
was first used by Albert Schweitzer. (Ed.)

possible to yield up every claim of one's own and submit obediently to the will of God. It is this way of the good will, that Jesus preached, which leads man directly to the awareness of his own unworthiness and worthlessness in the sight of God, and of his own situation as faced with inevitable decision; it is only here that he learns the profoundest meaning of God's forgiveness, which one can receive only as a little child.

(FROM: *Form Criticism*, Harper Torchbooks, 1962, pp. 20–4, 28–30, 32–5, 36–46, 71–4.)

2   THE OFFENCE OF THE INCARNATION

[Some of Bultmann's best writing has been on St John's gospel. A good example of this is the extract given here from his *Theology of the New Testament*. A first reading of St John's gospel might give the reader the impression that the enigmatic, ironic Christ of the synoptic tradition had disappeared, to be replaced by a Christ who openly reveals himself unambiguously from the start. Bultmann shows how even what might seem the most startling example of this, the miracles of St John, are in fact presented in a very 'misunderstandable', 'signful' way. There is a 'messianic secret' about the Christ of the fourth gospel, just as there is in the earlier tradition. Bultmann is also illuminating in the way he shows that the Christ of the fourth gospel is presented in language which is deliberately intended to carry a double-meaning, and suggest simultaneously both the historical Jesus of Nazareth and the present Christ of Christian belief.]

1. How does God's Son come into the world? As a human being. The theme of the whole Gospel of John is the statement: 'The word become flesh' (1:14). This statement is defended by I and II John against the false teachers. These are evidently Christian Gnostics[1] who deny the identity of the Son of God with the human Jesus either by asserting that their union was only temporary or by flatly rejecting the reality of the human

[1] Gnostics (literally 'those who know') tended to qualify or deny the real humanity of Christ (Ed.).

Jesus and docetically[1] regarding the human form of the Son of God as only a seeming body. John's answer to them is: every spirit that does not confess that Jesus Christ came in the flesh, that does not confess Jesus (the man as the Son of God) is not 'from God'; indeed, such false doctrine is nothing less than the work of Antichrist (I John 4:2 f.; II John 7). Just because John makes use of the Gnostic Redeemer-myth for his picture of the figure and activity of Jesus, a demarcation of his own position from that of Gnosticism is particularly incumbent upon him.

It is clear to begin with that for him the incarnation of the Son of God is not, as it is in Gnosticism, a cosmic event which sets into motion the eschatological occurrence (the unfolding of redemption) as a process of nature by which the union of the essentially opposite natures, light and darkness, is dissolved. The Gnostic Redeemer releases the pre-existent human selves, who by virtue of their light-nature are related to him, out of the matter (body and 'soul') that trammels them, and then leads them to the world of light above. John eliminated both the Gnostic concept of φύσις ('nature') and the Gnostic notion of the pre-existence of human selves and their unnatural imprisonment in the material world. He does not accept the Gnostic trichotomy of man, according to which man's true self is imprisoned in a body and a soul. Neither is the incarnation of the Son of God for John a device for transmitting 'Gnosis' to men in the form of teachings about cosmogony and anthropology or for bringing them secret formulas and sacraments, on the strength of which their selves can safely make the journey to heaven.

The Revealer appears not as man-in-general, i.e., not simply as a bearer of human nature, but as a definite human being in history: Jesus of Nazareth. His humanity is genuine humanity: 'the word became flesh.' Hence, John has no theory about the pre-existent one's miraculous manner of entry into the world nor about the manner of his union with the man Jesus. He knows neither the legend of the virgin birth[2] nor that of Jesus'

---

[1] See note in Vol. 1, p. 92.

[2] In some Latin witnesses to the text of John 1:13 'qui...natus est' (who...was born) is found instead of 'who...were born'; this is certainly a 'correcting' of the original text. (Ed.)

birth in Bethlehem—or if he knows of them, he will have nothing to do with them. Jesus comes from Nazareth, and this fact, offensive to 'the Jews', is emphasized (1:45; 7:52) rather than deprecated. 'The Jews', knowing Jesus' place of origin and his parents (7:27 f.; 6:42), are not in error as to the facts, but err in denying the claim of this Jesus of Nazareth to be the Revealer of God. They err not in the matter upon which they judge but in making a judgement at all κατὰ σάρκα (according to the 'flesh'—according to external appearances).

Neither does the Revealer appear as a mystagogue communicating teachings, formulas, and rites as if he himself were only a means to an end who could sink into unimportance to any who had received his 'Gnosis.' Though Jesus says in departing from the earth, 'I have manifested thy name to the men whom thou gavest me out of the world' (17:6; cf. v. 26), still he has imparted no information about God at all, any more than he has brought instruction about the origin of the world or the fate of the self. He does not communicate anything, but calls men to himself. Or when he promises a gift, he is, himself, that gift: he himself is the bread of life that he bestows (6:35); he himself is the light (8:12); he himself is life (11:25; 14:6).

Jesus, the Son of God who has become man, is a genuine man—which again does not mean that in his personality the divine became visible so as to fill men with enthusiasm and touch their feelings or to fascinate and overwhelm them. If that were the case, the divine would then be conceived of simply as the human exalted and intensified. But according to John, the divine is the very counter-pole to the human, with the result that it is a paradox, an offence, that the Word became flesh. As a matter of fact, the divinity of the figure of Jesus in John is completely lacking in visibility, and the disciples' relation to him as 'friends' (15:14 f.) is by no means conceived of as a personal relation of human friendship. It is the farewell discourses especially that strive to teach this distinction by making clear that the disciples will not achieve the right relation to him until he has departed from them—indeed, that he is not in the full sense the Revealer until he has been lifted up and glorified (see especially 14:28; 16:7).

2. In what sense, then, can it be said of the incarnate Word,

'We have beheld his glory' (1:14)? Is his human figure, so to speak, a translucent picture through which his divinity gleams? On first thought it might seem so, for many passages of the evangelist represent Jesus as the 'divine man' ($\theta\epsilon\hat{\imath}o\varsigma\ \dot{\alpha}\nu\acute{\eta}\rho$) in the Hellenistic sense—a man who has miraculous knowledge at his command, does miracles, and is immune to the plottings of his enemies.

It is as a 'divine man' that Jesus sees through the people he meets (Peter, 1:42; Nathanael, 1:47 f.) and knows the past of the Samaritan woman (4:17 f.). But to the evangelist these stories taken from tradition are symbolic pictures which indicate that the believer feels himself searched and known by God and that his own existence is exposed by the encounter with the Revealer. When 2:42 f., generalizing, says that Jesus sees through men, the author is not thinking of a supranatural ability but of the knowledge about man which arises from knowing God, and therefore knows what a stumbling-block God is to men. The same motif underlies the words, 'But I know that you have not the love of God within you' (5:42)—Jesus deduces this from the unbelief of the 'Jews'; he knows that face to face with the divine Revelation human resistance to God comes to light. Thus he knows that men mutter when they hear the Revealer's 'hard saying' (6:60 f.) and knows what oppresses believers and limits their comprehension, so long as they have not freed themselves from the notion that the Revelation ought to cause an alteration within this world (16:19).

Jesus' omniscience is confirmed by the disciples: 'Now we know that you know all things' (16:30)—but not because he has demonstrated it by miraculous knowledge, but because now at his farewell he has spoken 'plainly' ($\pi\alpha\rho\rho\eta\sigma\acute{\imath}\alpha$) without any 'figure' ($\pi\alpha\rho\omega\mu\acute{\imath}\alpha$, 'riddle,' 16:29). But in reality it is not some progress in Jesus' conduct that is characterized in the transition from 'riddles' to 'openness' but a change in the disciples' situation. For in the end Jesus has not said anything materially different from what he had always been saying, but what he had previously said now is seen in a new light; for in the light of Jesus' departure it now appears as something provisional for which only the future can bring a definite unveiling—that is to say, a genuine understanding (16:12–28, especially vv. 25 f.). The disciples' confession therefore anticipates this future and simply means that in Jesus' work as Revealer, which has now reached its end, all knowledge is contained. In keeping with this the confession continues not, 'and you need to question no one', but: 'And no one needs to question you.' The 'omniscience' of Jesus is therefore not understood to be his super-human ability, but his knowledge which is transmitted to the believer: whoever has recognized him as the Revealer by knowing that one thing knows everything, and Jesus' promise is fulfilled: 'On that day you will ask me no questions' (16:23).

The mention of Jesus' miraculous knowledge in the story of Lazarus is the result of unconsidered adoption of tradition (11:4, 11-14). Naturally, Jesus knows of his coming betrayal by Judas before the event (6:64, 70; 13:18). Perhaps this is due to an apologetic motif (if it is allowable even to look for such in this Gospel). But in addition to this possible motif, it is probably another idea that is dominant here: the idea that in the very nature of the Revelation—because it arouses man's resistance—there lies the possibility for the apostasy even of a disciple. Faith has no guarantee, and the Church must surmount the stumbling-block created by the fact that the devil finds his tool even in her own midst. Jesus' prediction of the disciples' flight and of persecution for the Church (16:32; 15:18-16:4a) is to be interpreted in a similar fashion: it is a foreknowledge which results from insight into the nature of the Revelation. That is also the way in which Jesus' knowledge of the fate that awaits him is to be understood. He is both the bringer of the Revelation and is himself the Revelation. Therefore he knows what is to befall him (2:19, 21); he knows 'the hour' (13:1; 18:4; 19:28). For him the perfect 'Gnostic' (i.e., knower), fate is no riddle.

Several times Jesus eludes harm or is snatched out of his enemies' hands until his hour is come (7:30, 44; 8:20, 59; 10:39). This motif has the purpose of demonstrating the fact that the Revealer's fate is not determined by human will but is in the hands of God.

3. Jesus performs miracles, a fact that is sometimes mentioned in general terms (2:23; 3:2; 4:45; 7:3, 31; 10:41, 11:47; 12:37; 20:30) and sometimes is depicted in accounts of specific miracles (2:1-12; 4:46-54; 5:1-9; 6:1-25; 9:1-7; 11:1-44).

The term used for these miracles is σημεῖα ('signs' and, secondarily, 'miracles'), and in John this word retains its true meaning of 'sign.' The 'signs' reveal Jesus' glory (2:11 cf. 9:3; 11:4), and the disbelief that refuses to be convinced by so many miracles is reproved (12:37). On the other hand, however, Jesus says in rebuke: 'Unless you see signs and wonders you will not believe' (4:48). And the risen Jesus addresses to Thomas the reproving word: 'Do you believe now because you have seen me? Blessed are those who see (me) not and yet believe' (20:29 tr.). It is an indication of disbelief when 'the Jews' ask: ('Then what sign do you do, that we may see, and believe you? What work do you perform)?' (6:30; cf. 2:18). They ask for a miracle analogous to the manna-miracle of Moses, and have no understanding of the work Jesus is performing. The fact that their question chronologically follows the sign of the bread-miracle makes it clear that the meaning of the sign does not lie in the miraculous occurrence. In fact, this had already been said in v. 26: 'You seek me, not because you saw signs, but because you ate some of the loaves and were filled' (6:26 tr.).

As 'signs' the miracles of Jesus are ambiguous. Like Jesus' words, they are misunderstandable. Of course, they are remarkable occurrences, but that only makes them indicators that the activity of the Revealer is a disturbance of what is familiar to the world. They point to the fact that the Revelation is no worldly occurrence, but an other-worldly one. They are pictures, symbols. The wine-miracle, an epiphany (2:1–12) symbolizes what occurs in all Jesus' work: the revelation of his 'glory'—not the glory of a miracle-worker, but that of him by whom the gift of 'grace and truth' is made. The cure of the official's son (4:46–54) and the healing of the lame man at the pool (5:1–9), both miraculous, are 'signs' only in the general sense that they point to the Revealer's work as of life-promoting kind. But the bread-miracle (6:1–15), the cure of the blind man (9:1–7), and the raising of Lazarus (11:1–44) have specific symbolic meaning: they represent the Revelation as food, light, and life respectively. It can hardly be decided whether the walking on the water is appended to the multiplication of the loaves only by the force of tradition or whether it is meant to convey that the Revealer and the Revelation are not subject to the laws of natural life.

We have already seen how 6:26 and 30 indicate that the 'signs,' though they are miraculous occurrences, do not furnish Jesus with legitimating credentials. The remark that the faith of the many, which rests upon the miracles, is no trustworthy faith (2:23-25) indicates the same thing. John's whole presentation shows, rather, that if the miracles are not understood as signs, they are an offence! The healing of the lame man and the cure of the blind man both elicit enmity and persecution, and the raising of Lazarus brings Jesus to the cross. The miracles may be for many the first shock that leads them to pay heed to Jesus and so begin to have faith—for this purpose, miracles are, so to speak, conceded; nevertheless, for the leaders of the people, the representatives of 'the world', the miracles are the offence that leads them to condemn him to death (11:47; cf. 12:18 f.).

4. Just because the miracles are 'signs' which require understanding, they also provide the possibility of misunderstanding. After the bread-miracle which raises the question whether he is 'the prophet who is to come into the world' (6:14), the crowd wants to make him king (6:15) because it expects material benefits of him (6:26). His brothers want to take him to Jerusalem to the Feast of Tabernacles so that he may make himself conspicuous there, saying: 'For no man works in secret if he seeks to be known openly. If you do these things, show yourself to the world' (7:4). They do not understand the way in which the Revelation works. They do not understand that from the world's standpoint the Revelation must always be a 'hidden thing' (cf. 'in secret' 7:4) and that it nevertheless occurs 'openly'—not, however, with demonstrative obtrusiveness but with the unobtrusiveness of everyday events. What is true of the miracles is true of all that Jesus does: it is not understood. Even the disciples understand the cleansing of the temple no more than 'the Jews' do. Not until after the resurrection does its meaning dawn upon them (2:17); likewise with the entry into Jerusalem (12:16). Peter does not grasp the meaning of the foot-washing (13:4 ff.).

As Jesus' actions are misunderstood, so are his words so long as they are conceived in the categories of worldly thought.

'The Jews' cannot but grossly misunderstand the saying about the destruction and rebuilding of the temple (2:20). As Nicodemus is able to understand re-birth only in the external natural sense (3:4), so the woman of Samaria misunderstands the saying about 'living water' first to mean running water and then to mean miraculous water (4:11, 15). The disciples cannot conceive what food Jesus means as his secret nourishment (4:33), nor can 'the Jews' guess what the bread from heaven is that Jesus bestows (6:34). Jesus' saying about his departure is misunderstood as an intention to go to the Dispersion (7:35 f.) or even to kill himself (8:22). The disciples misunderstand the sentence addressed to Judas: 'What you are going to do, do quickly' (13:27 f.). And Thomas cannot cope with the statement that the disciples know the way which Jesus will take (14:4). The disciples do not understand the 'little while' used by Jesus of his approaching departure and return (16:17 f.). They do not see why Jesus does not wish to manifest himself to the world (14:22). The incomprehension of the crowd is symbolically illustrated by the fact that some misunderstand the heavenly voice in answer to Jesus' prayer as thunder and others understand it as the angel voice which it is, but without perceiving that it is really speaking not to Jesus but to them (12:28–38).

In all these misunderstandings the offence of the assertion, 'the word became flesh' finds expression. This offence lies in the fact that the Revealer appears as a man whose claim to be the Son of God is one which he cannot, indeed, must not, prove to the world. For the Revelation is judgement upon the world and is necessarily felt as an attack upon it and an offence to it, so long as the world refuses to give up its norms. Until it does so, the world inevitably misunderstands the words and deeds of the Revealer, or they remain a riddle for it (10:6; 16:25, 29), even though Jesus has said everything openly all along (18:20). The world's inner capacity to understand comes most crassly to expression in the demand, 'If you are the Christ, tell us plainly'. Jesus, of course, had been telling them for a long time, so he can only answer, 'I told you, and you do not believe' (10:24 f.). Evidently he is to the world a foreigner whose language it does not understand. Why not? Not because he is not a real man, but because he, a mere man, demands credence for his claim to be the Revealer: 'Why do you not understand what I say? Because you cannot hear my word' (8:43 tr.). Why do 'the Jews' who know him and his home town, nevertheless not know who he is nor where he comes from? Because they do not know God (7:28) ! So, on the one hand, Jesus can say that he does not bear witness for himself; if he did, his testimony would not be true (5:31 f.). On the other hand, he is constantly bearing witness for himself by claiming to be the Revealer, and can assert that his testimony is true when he does so (8:14). Each statement is true, according to which point of view is adopted: such a testimony as the world demands, a legitimation, he cannot and must not give. But there is a testimony which consists of his claim to be the Revealer, a claim which denies the world's competence to judge; in the world's opinion this cannot be considered true testimony (8:13). But this testimony he must bear.

The offence of the assertion 'the word became flesh', comes most clearly to light in the direct contradiction of Jesus' claim. It can only appear as an insane blasphemy that he, a man, makes himself equal to God, and the authorities seek to kill him (5:17 f.). His claim calls forth the accusation that he is demon-possessed and a 'Samaritan' (8:51 f.). So does his assertion that whoever keeps his word will not see death (8:51 f.). And when he claims that he is older than Abraham (8:57), they want to stone him (8:59). His assertion that he and the Father are one fills them with such indignation that once more they want to stone him (10:30 f.). In short, his 'hard word' is intolerable to hear. And his persistence in his claim results in the apostasy of all but a few of his very disciples (6:66). What a scandal (σκάνδαλον) his cross will one day be to men, he hints in the words: 'Does this (his "hard word") scandalize you? What, then, if you see the Son of Man ascending where he was at first?' (6:61 f., tr.)—a saying of remarkably double meaning, for the world will, of course, perceive only the outward form of his 'ascending': his crucifixion. John at the end brings this *skandalon* drastically into view when he has Pilate present the scourged and thorn-crowned Jesus to the crowd with the words, 'Behold the man!' (19:5) and, 'Behold your king!' (19:14). Here and in the incription over the cross (19:19) the paradoxical stumbling-block of

Jesus' claim is presented in a symbol of tremendous irony.
5. By his presentation of Jesus' work as the incarnate Son of
God John has singularly developed and deepened Mark's
theory of the Messiah-secret[1] (4, 4). Over the figure of Jesus
there hangs a mystery, even though—or rather just because—
he quite openly says who he is and what claim he makes. For
to the world he is still in spite of all publicity the hidden
Messiah, not because he conceals anything or commands anything to be kept secret, but because the world does not see with
seeing eyes (12:40). His hiddenness is the very consequence of
his self-revelation; his revealing of himself is the very thing
that makes 'those who see' become 'blind' (9:39).

His work as a whole, which forms a unity framed by his
coming and his departure, is both revelation and offence. His
departure or 'exaltation' (i.e., upon the cross) not only belongs
to the whole as its culmination but is that which makes the
whole what it is: both revelation and offence. The possibility
considered by Jesus in the meditation which is John's substitute for the Gethsemane scene of the synoptic tradition, 'What
shall I say? "Father, save me from this hour"?' Jesus immedi-
ately rejects: 'No, for this purpose I have come to this hour'
(12:27). In his passion the meaning of the sending of Jesus is
fulfilled. And by his conceiving and accepting it as the fulfilment of the mission enjoined upon him by the Father (14:31),
it becomes the hours of exaltation, the hour of glorification.
Seen from the vantage-point of this fulfilment the whole work
of the man Jesus is a revelation of the divine glory. Whereas
in the Gospel of Mark we can recognize the historical process
by which the unmessianic life of Jesus was retrospectively made
messianic, in John the inner appropriateness of that process is
made clear. This is expressed by the evangelist by means of the
petition of Jesus which follows the deliberation mentioned
above: 'Father, glorify thy name' (12:28) and by the heavenly
voice which answers this prayer, 'I have glorified it, and I will
glorify it again' (12:28). Hence, the glorification of God's
name which begins with Jesus' exaltation by crucifixion and
the glorification of God's name by the ministry of the earthly
Jesus (17:4) are a unity. Neither exists without the other; each
exists only through the other. But the glorification of the name

[1] See p. 38.

of God is also the glorification of Jesus himself, and Jesus' other prayer, 'Father, the hour has come; glorify thy Son' (17:1), corresponds to this one ('Father, glorify thy name'). And the motive for this prayer—'that the Son may glorify thee'—makes the unity of God's glory and Jesus' glory evident. And when the motive is further developed in the words 'since thou hast given him power over all flesh' (17:2), the unity of his glory after the exaltation with that before it is once again made clear. Both unities are once more expressed in the words which pronounce the granting of this prayer:

'Now is the Son of man glorified,
   and in him God is glorified;
if God is glorified in him,
   God will also glorify him in himself
and glorify him at once' (13:31 f.).

In the 'now' of the 'hour' when the Son of God departs from the world the past and the future are bound together, as it were. And since not until the future will the past be made into what it really is (viz., the revelation of the 'glory'), the disciples can only be glad that Jesus is going away (14:28; 16:7).

Faith in Jesus, then, is faith in the exalted Jesus, but not as if he were a heavenly being who had stripped off the garment of earthly-human existence as the Gnostic Redeemer was conceived to do. Rather, the exalted Jesus is at the same time the earthly man Jesus; the 'glorified one' is still always he who 'became flesh'. In other words, Jesus' life on earth does not become an item of the historical past, but constantly remains present reality. The historical figure of Jesus, i.e., his human history, retains its significance of being the revelation of his 'glory' and thereby of God's. It is the eschatological occurrence. Of course, this is not visible to the world, for the exalted Jesus does not reveal himself to it (14:22)—indeed he cannot, for it cannot receive the Spirit of truth which gives knowledge to those who believe (14:17; 16:13 f.). But those who believe can now look back upon Jesus' earthly life and say, 'We have beheld his glory (1:14).

(FROM: *Theology of the New Testament*, London 1955, Volume II, pp. 40–9.)

3 DEMYTHOLOGIZING

[Bultmann's work as a form-critic made him sceptical about what one could say with certainty about the historical Jesus, beyond the fact that he existed, the 'Christ-event'. The latter he believed still had unique and vital significance but unfortunately it was clothed by the New Testament writers in 'mythological' terms. In the first extract given here, originally a talk broadcast by the BBC, Bultmann explains why he thinks the New Testament material must be 'demythologized' and re-presented in a way which is 'independent of every picture of the world'.

The second extract gives a sample of the kind of 'demythologizing the event of Christ', especially the crucifixion and resurrection, which commends itself to Bultmann. Readers will find it instructive to compare this with Tillich's treatment of the crucifixion and resurrection in Vol. 3. pp. 92 ff.]

(a) *What is Demythologizing?*

What does 'demythologizing the Bible' mean? There are many passages in the Bible, especially those about God and God's action which for the thought of modern man bear the stamp of mythological expressions. To demythologize does not mean to eliminate those passages, but rather to make them understandable to modern thought. Demythologizing is not a process of subtraction, but a method of interpreting Scripture. It is a method which questions the mythological expressions of Scripture about the truth they contain, because the mythological form in which this truth is clothed makes the passages incomprehensible to modern thought. For this is, in fact, the state of affairs; people today find the statements of the Bible largely incomprehensible, and therefore reject them with scorn or indifference, just because they are clothed in the forms of mythological thinking.

A stumbling block

A simple example will make this clear. In mythological thinking, heaven above us is looked upon as God's dwelling-place. The truth intended to be expressed by this is that God does not belong to this earthly world: he is superior to it, beyond it, he is transcendent. Mythological thinking assumes that it is possible to express God's transcendence by using spatial thought-forms of infinite distance, of a place high above us. The question arises whether it is not necessary to express the truth contained in the thought of God's transcendence in other thought-forms for modern man, because he has ceased to think mythologically. So he may not be able to understand what is really meant when the Bible speaks about God in heaven, and about Christ's ascension and sitting at the right hand of God. And just as we must demythologize the image of the ascension, in order to preserve its truth, so, too, with the image of the descent into hell. For the mythological concept of hell aims similarly at expressing the transcendent power of evil and the transcendence of man's lost state when he is without God. It does this with the aid of an inadequate spatial image, in which the transcendence which is hostile to God is localized in the depths. But who really believes today that hell is in the depths, underneath the ground we tread? The image of above and below can no longer be applied to the contemporary picture of the universe. And is the stumbling block, which the Christian message is meant to provide to men, to consist in its asking them to accept an out-of-date picture of the world?

It is sometimes said that the mythological forms of the Bible are after all just pictures, and as a matter of fact the Bible does make use of mythological forms as pictures. But we must be clear that when this does happen, then demythologizing has already begun. And we must be consistent, and above all we must be quite responsible in our choice of images and concepts, to formulate properly the truth which is contained in the mythological pictures.

The illustrations of heaven and hell make clear to us the characteristic element in mythological thinking. Thus it is not sufficient to oppose mythological to rational thinking. For a myth always contains a point of rational thinking, as well—otherwise it would not be thinking at all. And there are myths which can be described as primitive science—for example, those which try to explain striking natural phenomena such as eclipses of the sun and moon. The distinction between myth and science is that myth deals with a different reality from science. The real purpose of myth—at least in the sphere of religion—is to speak of the powers, or the power, which sets a limit to man's thinking, willing, and doing, that is, the power on which man's existence depends, by whose favour or grace he lives, before whose wrath or judgement he trembles; the power, in short, which is not a part of the world managed by man, or at least managed by his knowledge, but is supernatural, beyond this world. But myth speaks of this power beyond the world in an insufficient way, when it presents transcendence as distant in space, above or beneath the earth, and when it thinks of the transcendent other-worldly power as a this-worldly power raised to enormous magnitude. This way of thinking, contrary to the intention of the myth, turns the other-worldly into something in this world; it turns the gods into a kind of super-men. Even when myth speaks of God's omnipotence and omniscience, it speaks mythologically since it makes only a quantitative and not a qualitative distinction between God's omnipotence and omniscience and human power and knowledge.

You can say that mythological thinking turns God and transcendence into this-worldly objects, and as far as it does this it is akin to scientific thinking as far as scientific thinking objectifies the world and its phenomena, that is, tries to grasp their real nature. Demythologizing is against this objectifying thought which claims that it can understand divine existence in terms of this world. Demythologizing rests upon the insight that we are unable to speak of transcendence and God as they really are, since any attempt to do so would turn them into a phenomenon of this world. Demythologizing proceeds in accordance with the words of Melanchthon when he said: 'To know Christ is to know His benefits, not to look upon His nature.' Or, as Wilhelm Hermann, a theologian of the last generation, has put it: 'We cannot say what God is like in Himself, but only what He does to us.' So the aim of demythologizing is to understand the truth of the biblical utterances as a reality which meets our existence, and to express that truth in a way which is comprehensible to modern man. You can describe this demythologizing interpretation of the Bible as existential; but the name is not important. The important thing is that the words of the Bible, which in their mythological form have become incomprehensible to the man of today, should be made comprehensible. And this can be done by showing how the truth of the words meets our existence, how it discloses our existence to us, how it radically deepens the questions which consciously or unconsciously are stirring our existence, and how, lastly, it lays bare our illusions and our flight from God.

Do I need, after this, to defend demythologizing from the reproach that it tries to make the Gospel acceptable to science? Its aim is not in the least to make God and His actions into objects, into phenomena of this world. But its aim is to make the Gospel comprehensible as a call addressed to us, and comprehensible not for rational thinking but for existential self-understanding. Can it then be said that it assesses the Gospel in terms of the scientific picture of the world—and worse, the science of the last century? Not at all: at most we can say that the biblical picture of the world, but not the truth of the Gospel itself, is assessed in terms of the modern picture of the world. For the truth of the Gospel is independent of any picture of the world.

A truth independent of pictures

When I demythologize the Bible I reckon with the fact that the thinking of modern man has ceased to be mythological and is determined by science. For modern man lives in a world in which life makes constant use of technical means which have been created by science. When we are ill we have recourse to medical science; in economics and politics we make sensible use of the findings of psychology, sociology, economic science, and so on. We no longer reckon with the direct break-in of transcendent powers. In urging that the Bible be demythologized, I am well aware that modern science is very different from nineteenth-century science; nor do I deceive myself about the findings of science, all of which are relative and productive neither today nor in earlier generations of any final scientific picture of the world. But it is equally clear that the method of scientific thought and research is the same today as it has always been, at least since the rise of science in ancient Greece. In the course of Western history this method of thought has pushed mythological thinking to one side; and it would be illusory to try to revive it. Such a revival would not in the least help us to know the truth of the Gospel; for this truth is independent of every picture of the world.

If demythologizing tries to make comprehensible the biblical truth which has become incomprehensible in its mythological garments, does that mean that the truth is rationalized in the sense of being reduced to a product of rational thought? Certainly not. But the Christian truth and the mystery of God are meant to be understood; and understanding is not identical with rational explanation. A comparison may make clear what I mean. I can understand what friendship and love and loyalty mean; but that does not mean that the friendship and love and loyalty that I meet with—that I am given—in the course of my life do not remain a gratefully accepted mystery. I do not know these things by means of rational thought, but in the existential openness of my person. Again, I can understand what the grace of God means, otherwise I could not speak about it as I do. But the fact that this grace meets me is a mystery which has no rational explanation. Unless I understand the Word of God's grace in Christ I cannot believe in that Word; and demythologizing is concerned to make this Word understandable.

One of the biblical concepts which has become largely incomprehensible to modern man is the concept of sin. Perhaps it escapes a superficial study how strongly coloured this concept is by mythological thought, as, for example, when the devil is spoken of as the creator of sin, or when sin is represented as a power brought upon mankind by the fall of Adam. Demythologizing is concerned to make clear the depths of sin as our own guilt and at the same time as a power to which we are subservient and against which we are defenceless. Demythologizing is further concerned to make clear that freedom from sin means freedom for the future. If you think it is too meagre a definition of Christian faith to call it free openness for the future, then you must reflect what this definition includes. Is not the freedom which is given to us by the forgiveness of our sins the freedom from our past which weighs upon us and enslaves us? And is not the most certain thing in our future the certainty of death? Then openness for the future means the same as Paul did in his triumphant cry: 'Death is swallowed up in victory !'

(FROM: *The Listener*, 5 February 1953, pp. 217–18.)

(b) Demythologizing the Event of Christ

... Now, it is beyond question that the New Testament presents the event of Jesus Christ in mythical terms. The problem is whether that is the only possible presentation. Or does the New Testament itself demand a restatement of the event of Jesus Christ in nonmythological terms? Now, it is clear from the outset that the event of Christ is of a wholly different order from the cultmyths of Greek or Hellenistic religion. Jesus Christ is certainly presented as the Son of God, a pre-existent divine being, and therefore to that extent a mythical figure. But he is also a concrete figure of history—Jesus of Nazareth. His life is more than a mythical event; it is a human life which ended in the tragedy of crucifixion. We have here a unique combination of history and myth. The New Testament claims that this Jesus of history, whose father and mother were well known to his contemporaries (John 6 : 42) is at the same time the pre-existent Son of God, and side by side with the historical event of the crucifixion it sets the definitely non-historical event of the resurrection. This combination of myth and history presents a number of difficulties, as can be seen from certain inconsistencies in the New Testament material. The doctrine of Christ's pre-existence as given by St Paul and St John is difficult to reconcile with the legend of the Virgin birth in St Matthew and St Luke. On the one hand we hear that 'he emptied himself, taking the form of a servant, being made in the likeness of men: and being found in fashion as a man ...' (Phil. 2 : 7), and on the other hand we have the gospel portraits of a Jesus who manifests his divinity in his miracles, omniscience, and mysterious elusiveness, and the similar description of him in Acts as 'Jesus of Nazareth, a man approved of God unto you by mighty works and wonders and signs' (Acts 2 : 22). On the one hand we have the resurrection as the exaltation of Jesus from the cross or grave, and on the other the legends of the empty tomb and the ascension.

We are compelled to ask whether all this mythological language is not simply an attempt to express the meaning of the historical figure of Jesus and the events of his life; in other words, the significance of these as a figure and event of salvation. If that be so, we can dispense with the objective form in which they are cast.

It is easy enough to deal with the doctrine of Christ's pre-existence and the legend of the Virgin birth in this way. They are clearly attempts to explain the meaning of the Person of Jesus for faith. The facts which historical criticism can verify cannot exhaust, indeed they cannot adequately indicate, all that Jesus means to me. How he actually originated matters little, indeed we can appreciate his significance only when we cease to worry about such questions. Our interests in the events of his life, and above all in the cross, is more than an acedemic concern with the history of the past. We can see meaning in them only when we ask what God is trying to say to each one of us through them. Again, the figure of Jesus cannot be understood simply from his context in human evolution or history. In mythological language, this means that he stems from eternity, his origin transcends both history and nature.

We shall not, however, pursue the examination of the particular incidents of his life any further. In the end the crux of the matter lies in the cross and resurrection.

The Cross

Is the cross, understood as the event of redemption, exclusively mythical in character, or can it retain its value for salvation without forefeiting its character as history?

It certainly has a mythical character as far as its objective setting is concerned. The Jesus who was crucified was the pre-existent, incarnate Son of God, and as such he was without sin. He is the victim whose blood atones for our sins. He bears vicariously the sin of the world, and by enduring the punishment for sin on our behalf he delivers us from death. This mythological interpretation is a hotch-potch of sacrificial and juridical analogies, which have ceased to be tenable for us today. And in any case they fail to do justice to what the New Testament is trying to say. For the most they can convey is that the cross effects the forgiveness of all the past and future sins of man, in the sense that the punishment they deserved has been remitted. But the New Testament means more than this. The cross releases men not only from the guilt, but also from the power of sin. That is why, when the author of Colossians says 'He (God) . . . having forgiven us all our trespasses, having blotted out the bond written in ordinances that was against us, which was contrary to us; and he hath taken it out of the way, nailing it to the cross' he hastens to add: 'having put off from himself the principalities and powers, he made a show of them openly, triumphing over them in it' (Col. 2:13–15).

The historical event of the cross acquires cosmic dimensions and so its full significance is brought into sharper relief. For if we see in the cross the judgement of the world and the defeat of the rulers of this world (1 Cor. 2:6 ff.), the cross becomes the judgement of ourselves as fallen creatures enslaved to the powers of the 'world'.

By giving up Jesus to be crucified, God has set up the cross for us. To believe in the cross of Christ does not mean to concern ourselves with a mythical process wrought outside of us and our world, or with an objective event turned by God to our advantage, but rather to make the cross of Christ our own, to undergo crucifixion with him. The cross in its redemptive aspect is not an isolated incident which befell a mythical personage, but an event of 'cosmic' importance. Its decisive, revolutionary significance is brought out by the eschatological framework in which it is set. In other words, the cross is not just an event of the past which can be contemplated in detachment, but the eschatological event in and beyond time, for as far as its meaning—that is, its meaning for faith—is concerned, it is an ever-present reality.

The cross becomes a present reality in the sacraments. In baptism men and women are baptized into Christ's death (Rom. 6:3) and crucified with him (Rom. 6:6). At every celebration of the Lord's Supper the death of Christ is proclaimed (1 Cor. 11:26); The communicants thereby partake of his crucified body and his blood outpoured (1 Cor. 10:16).

Again, the cross of Christ is an ever-present reality in the every-day life of the Christians. 'They that are of Christ Jesus have crucified the flesh with the passions and the lusts thereof' (Gal. 5:24). That is why St Paul can speak of 'the cross of our Lord Jesus Christ, through which the world hath been crucified unto me, and I unto the world' (Gal. 6:14). That is why he seeks to know 'the fellowship of his sufferings', as one who is 'conformed to his death' (Phil. 3:10).

The crucifying of the affections and lusts includes the overcoming of our natural dread of suffering and the perfection of our detachment from the world. Hence the willing acceptance of sufferings in which death is already at work in man means: 'always bearing about in our body the dying of Jesus' and 'always being delivered unto death for Jesus' sake' (2 Cor. 4:10 f.).

Thus the cross and passion are ever-present realities. How little they are confined to the events of the first Good Friday is amply illustrated by the words which a disciple of St Paul puts into his master's mouth: 'Now I rejoice in my sufferings for your sake, and fill up on my part that which is lacking of the afflictions of Christ in my flesh for his body's sake, which is the Church' (Col. 1:24).

In its redemptive aspect the cross of Christ is no mere mythical event, but a permanent historical fact originating in the past historical event which is the crucifixion of Jesus. The abiding significance of the cross is that it is the judgement of the world, the judgement and the deliverance of man. In this sense Christ is crucified 'for us', a phrase which does not necessarily imply any theory of sacrifice or satisfaction. This interpretation of the cross as a permanent fact rather than a mythological event does far more justice to the redemptive significance of the event of the past than any of the traditional interpretations. In the last resort mythological language is only a medium for conveying the meanings of the past event. The real meaning of the cross is that it has created a new and permanent situation in history. The preaching of the cross as the event of redemption challenges all who hear it to appropriate this significance for themselves, to be willing to be crucified with Christ.

But, it will be asked, is this significance to be discerned in the actual event of past history? Can it, so to speak, be read off from that event? Or does the cross bear this significance because it is the cross of Christ? In other words, must we first be convinced of the significance of Christ and believe in him in order to discern the real meaning of the cross? If we are to perceive the real meaning of the cross, must we understand it as the cross of Jesus as a figure of past history? Must we go back to the Jesus of history?

As far as the first preachers of the gospel are concerned this will certainly be the case. For them the cross was the cross of him with whom they had lived in personal intercourse. The cross was an experience of their own lives. It presented them with a question and it disclosed to them its meaning. But for us this personal connexion cannot be reproduced. For us the cross cannot disclose its own meaning: it is an event of the past. We can never recover it as an event in our own lives. All we know of it is derived from historical report. But the New Testament does not proclaim Jesus Christ in this way. The meaning of the cross is not disclosed from the life of Jesus as a figure of past history, a life which needs to be reproduced by historical research. On the contrary, Jesus is not proclaimed merely as the crucified; he is also risen from the dead. The cross and the resurrection form an inseparable unity.

The Resurrection

But what of the resurrection? Is it not a mythical event pure and simple? Obviously it is not an event of past history with a self-evident meaning. Can the resurrection narrative and every other mention of the resurrection in the New Testament be understood simply as an attempt to convey the meaning of the cross? Does the New Testament, in asserting that Jesus is risen from the dead, mean that his death is not just an ordinary human death, but the judgement and salvation of the world, depriving death of its power? Does it not express this truth in the affirmation that the Crucified was not holden of death, but rose from the dead?

Yes indeed: the cross and the resurrection form a single, indivisible cosmic event. 'He was delivered up for our trespasses, and was raised for our justification' (Rom. 4:25). The cross is not an isolated event, as though it were the end of

Jesus, which needed the resurrection subsequently to reverse
it When he suffered death, Jesus was already the Son of God,
and his death by itself was the victory over the power of death.
St John brings this out most clearly by describing the passion
of Jesus as the 'hour' in which he is glorified, and by the double
meaning he gives to the phrase 'lifted up', applying it both to
the cross and to Christ's exaltation into glory.

Cross and resurrection form a single, indivisible cosmic
event which brings judgement to the world and opens up for
men the possibility of authentic life. But if that be so, the
resurrection cannot be a miraculous proof capable of demonstration and sufficient to convince the sceptic that the cross
really has the cosmic and eschatological significance ascribed
to it.

Yet it cannot be denied that the resurrection of Jesus is often
used in the New Testament as a miraculous proof. Take for
instance Acts 17:31. Here we are actually told that God
substantiated the claims of Christ by raising him from the
dead. Then again the resurrection narratives: both the legend
of the empty tomb and the appearances insist on the physical
reality of the risen body of the Lord (see especially Luke 24:
39–43). But these are most certainly later embellishments of
the primitive tradition. St Paul knows nothing about them.
There is, however, one passage where St Paul tries to prove
the miracle of the resurrection by adducing a list of eye-
witnesses (1 Cor. 15:3–8). But this is a dangerous procedure,
as Karl Barth has involuntarily shown. Barth seeks to explain
away the real meaning of 1 Cor. 15 by contending that the list
of eye-witnesses was put in not to prove the fact of the resurrection, but to prove that the preaching of the apostle was,
like the preaching of the first Christians, the preaching of Jesus
as the risen Lord. The eye-witnesses therefore guarantee St
Paul's preaching, not the fact of the resurrection. An historical
fact which involves a resurrection from the dead is utterly
inconceivable !

Yes indeed: the resurrection of Jesus cannot be a miraculous proof by which the sceptic might be compelled to believe
in Christ. The difficulty is not simply the incredibility of a
mythical event like the resuscitation of a corpse—for that is
what the resurrection means, as is shown by the fact that the

risen Lord is apprehended by the physical senses. Nor is it merely the difficulty of establishing the objective historicity of the resurrection no matter how many witnesses are cited, as though once it was established it might be believed beyond all question and faith might have its unimpeachable guarantee. No; the real difficulty is that the resurrection is itself an article of faith, and you cannot establish one article of faith by invoking another. You cannot prove the redemptive efficacy of the cross by invoking the resurrection. For the resurrection is an article of faith because it is far more than the resuscitation of a corpse—it is the eschatological event. And so it cannot be a miraculous proof. For, quite apart from its credibility, the bare miracle tells us nothing about the eschatological fact of the destruction of death. Moreover, such a miracle is not otherwise unknown to mythology.

It is however abundantly clear that the New Testament is interested in the resurrection of Christ simply and solely because it is the eschatological event par excellence. By it Christ abolished death and brought life and immortality to light (2 Tim. 1:10). This explains why St Paul borrows Gnostic language to clarify the meaning of the resurrection. As in the death of Jesus all have died (2 Cor. 5:14 f.), so through his resurrection all have been raised from the dead, though naturally this event is spread over a long period of time (1 Cor. 15:21 f.). But St Paul does not only say: 'In Christ shall all be made alive'; he can also speak of rising again with Christ in the present tense, just as he speaks of our dying with him. Through the sacrament of baptism Christians participate not only in the death of Christ but also in his resurrection. It is not simply that we shall walk with him in newness of life and be united with him in his resurrection (Rom. 6:4 f.); we are doing so already here and now. 'Even so reckon ye yourselves to be dead indeed unto sin, but alive unto God in Jesus Christ' (Rom. 6:11).

Once again, in everyday life the Christians participate not only in the death of Christ but also in his resurrection. In this resurrection-life they enjoy a freedom, albeit a struggling freedom, from sin (Rom. 6:11 ff.). They are able to 'cast off the works of darkness', so that the approaching day when the darkness shall vanish is already experienced here and now. 'Let us walk honestly as in the day' (Rom. 13:12 f.): 'we are not of the night, nor of the darkness ... Let us, since we are of the day, be sober ...' (1 Thess. 5:5–8). St Paul seeks to share not only the sufferings of Christ but also 'the power of his resurrection' (Phil. 3:10). So he bears about in his body the dying of Jesus, 'that the life also of Jesus may be manifested in our body' (2 Cor. 4:10 f.). Similarly, when the Corinthians demand a proof of his apostolic authority, he solemnly warns them: 'Christ is not weak, but is powerful in you: for he was crucified in weakness, yet he liveth in the power of God. For we also are weak in him, but we shall live with him through the power of God toward you' (2 Cor. 13:3 f.).

In this way the resurrection is not a mythological event adduced in order to prove the saving efficacy of the cross, but an article of faith just as much as the meaning of the cross itself. Indeed, faith in the resurrection is really the same thing as faith in the saving efficacy of the cross, faith in the cross as the cross of Christ. Hence you cannot first believe in Christ and then in the strength of that faith believe in the cross. To believe in Christ means to believe in the cross as the cross of Christ. The saving efficacy of the cross is not derived from the fact that it is the cross of Christ: it is the cross of Christ because it has this saving efficacy. Without that efficacy it is the tragic end of a great man.

We are back again at the old question. How do we come to believe in the cross as the cross of Christ and as the eschatological event par excellence? How do we come to believe in the saving efficacy of the cross?

There is only one answer. This is the way in which the cross is proclaimed. It is always proclaimed together with the resurrection. Christ meets us in the preaching as one crucified and risen. He meets us in the word of preaching and nowhere else. The faith of Easter is just this—faith in the word of preaching.

It would be wrong at this point to raise again the problem of how this preaching arose historically, as though that could vindicate its truth. That would be to tie our faith in the word of God to the results of historical research. The word of preaching confronts us as the word of God. It is not for us to question its credentials. It is we who are questioned, we who are asked whether we will believe the word or reject it. But answering this question, in accepting the word of preaching as the word of God and the death and resurrection of Christ as the eschatological event, we are given an opportunity of understanding ourselves. Faith and unbelief are never blind, arbitrary decisions. They offer us the alternative between accepting or rejecting that which alone can illuminate our understanding of ourselves.

The real Easter faith is faith in the word of preaching which brings illumination. If the event of Easter Day is in any sense an historical event additional to the event of the cross, it is nothing else than the rise of faith in the risen Lord, since it was this faith which led to the apostolic preaching. The resurrection itself is not an event of past history. All that historical criticism can establish is the fact that the first disciples came to believe in the resurrection. The historian can perhaps to some extent account for that faith from the personal intimacy which the disciples had enjoyed with Jesus during his earthly life, and so reduce the resurrection appearances to a series of subjective visions. But the historical problem is scarcely relevant to Christian belief in the resurrection. For the historical event of the rise of the Easter faith means for us what it meant for the first disciples—namely, the self-manifestation of the risen Lord, the act of God in which the redemptive event of the cross is completed.[1]

We cannot buttress our own faith in the resurrection by that of the first disciples and so eliminate the element of risk which faith in the resurrection always involves. For the first disciples' faith in the resurrection is itself part and parcel of the eschatological event which is the article of faith.

In other words, apostolic preaching which originated in the event of Easter Day is itself a part of the eschatological event of redemption. The death of Christ, which is both the judgement and the salvation of the world, inaugurates the 'ministry of reconciliation' or 'word of reconciliation' (2 Cor. 5:18 f.). This word supplements the cross and makes its saving efficacy

[1] This and the following paragraphs are also intended as an answer to the doubts and suspicions which Paul Althaus has raised against me in *Die Wahrheit des kirchlichen Osterglaubens*, 1941, p. ff. Cp. also my discussion of Emanuel Hirsch's 'Die Auferstehungsgeschichten und der christliche Glaube', 1940, in *Theol. Lit.-Ztg.*, 1940, pp. 242-6.

intelligible by demanding faith and confronting men with the
question whether they are willing to understand themselves as
men who are crucified and risen with Christ. Through the word
of preaching the cross and the resurrection are made present:
the eschatological 'now' is here, and the promise of Isaiah
49:8 is fulfilled: 'Behold, now is the acceptable time; behold,
now is the day of salvation' (2 Cor. 6:2). That is why the
apostolic preaching brings judgement. For some the apostle is
'a savour from death unto death' and for others 'a savour
from life unto life' (2 Cor. 2:16). St Paul is the agent through
whom the resurrection life becomes effective in the faithful
(2 Cor. 4:12). The promise of Jesus in the Fourth Gospel is
eminently applicable to the preaching in which he is proclaimed: 'Verily I say unto you, He that heareth my words
and believeth on him that sent me, hath eternal life, and
cometh not unto judgement, but hath passed out of death into
life . . . The hour cometh and now is, when the dead shall hear
the voice of the Son of God; and they that hear shall live'
(John 5:24 f.). In the word of preaching and there alone we
meet the risen Lord. 'So belief cometh of hearing, and hearing
by word of Christ' (Rom. 10:17).

Like the word itself and the apostle who proclaims it, so the
Church where the preaching of the word is continued and
where the believers or 'saints' (i.e., those who have been trans-
ferred to eschatological existence) are gathered is part of the
eschatological event. The word 'Church' ($\dot{\epsilon}\kappa\kappa\lambda\eta\sigma\dot{\iota}\alpha$) is an
eschatological term, while its designation as the Body of Christ
emphasizes its cosmic significance. For the Church is not just
a phenomenon of secular history, it is a phenomenon of significant history, in the sense that it realizes itself in history.

(FROM: *Kerygma and Myth* I, edited by H.-W. Bartsch,
London 1957, pp. 34–43.)

4   THE IDEA OF GOD AND MODERN MAN

[In this extract we have Bultmann's reaction to the debate started by the Bishop of Woolwich's *Honest to God*. This centred on the use of metaphor in religious language, and the meaning to be attached to the 'transcendence' of God. Bultmann also touches on the 'death of God' theology in the United States (William Hamilton, Thomas J. J. Altizer and others, see introduction pp. 29 ff.) and in doing so provides an illuminating pedigree of contemporary atheism.]

At the beginning of 1963 there appeared the book of the Anglican bishop, John A. T. Robinson, *Honest to God* (honest to and about God).[1] In both England and Germany (as well as in America) it has provoked a somewhat heated debate. Articles appeared in the Hamburg newspaper, *Die Zeit*, with captions 'Is God a metaphor?', 'Is our image of God dated?', 'Is faith in God finished?'—questions evoked by Robinson's book. Some theologians rightly observed that the ideas advanced by Robinson were not new in contemporary theology. Now Robinson had not made this claim at all. He calls repeatedly on Paul Tillich, Dietrich Bonhoeffer and others.[2] But in the process of assimilating their thought, he sees that they add up to the following sum, so to speak: *a revolution is necessary*. For, since the traditional ecclesiastical image of God is no longer credible to contemporary men, *a new image of God* is required; the old one is obsolete.

It is understandable that for many readers—especially for readers among the laity to whom the book is directed—this thesis is frightening. With the disposal of the old image of God, is not faith in God and thereby also God himself finished? That this question forces itself upon men today is not signalized by Robinson's book alone. As early as 1961 there appeared

---

[1] SCM Press (England), Westminster Press (U.S.A.), 1963.

[2] Professor Bultmann's modesty prevents him from mentioning that Robinson also calls frequently on him. (Trs.)

the book, *The Death of God*,[1] by the American theologian, Gabriel Vahanian, which is a peculiar and admittedly theologically independent parallel to Robinson's book. The title of Vahanian's book comes from the famous pronouncement of Nietzsche[2]: 'God is dead.'

The note 'God is dead' was struck almost a hundred years before Nietzsche by Jean Paul[3] in his *Siebenkäs*, which appeared in 1796-7, and there is a ghastly vision: 'Discourse of the dead Christ from atop the cosmos: there is no God.'[4] This discourse is not a philosophical discussion of atheism. The import of the vision consists rather in showing that atheism is nihilism (in this respect also a precursor of Nietzsche): 'The whole universe is burst asunder by the hand of atheism and fragmented into innumerable quick-silver particles of I's, which twinkle, roll about, wander, flee together and from each other without unity and stability. No one is so very much alone in the universe as the one who denies God ... Alas, if every I is its own father and creator, why can it not also be its own angel of destruction?'

Nietzsche permits the 'madman' to proclaim the message of the death of God in his work *Die fröhiche Wissenschaft* (1881). Martin Heidegger says in his essay 'Nietzsches Wort "God ist tot"'[5]: 'Nietzsche's word spells the destiny of two thousand years of Western history.' This remarkable assertion rests on

[1] G. Vahanian, *The Death of God*. The Culture of our Post-Christian Era, New York, George Braziller, 1961. By the same author, *Beyond the Death of God:* The Need of Cultural Revolution, Dialog 1, 4, 1962, pp. 18–21.

[2] Friedrich Nietzsche (1844–1900). German philosopher and poet. The phrase 'God is dead' comes in his *The Gay Science*. (Ed.)

[3] 'Jean Paul' the pseudonym of Johann Paul Friedrich Richter (1763–1825), German novelist. (Ed.)

[4] G. Bornkamm has reprinted the speech as an appendix to the second volume of his collected essays: *Studien zu Antike und Urchristentum*, Gesammelte Aufsätze II. (Beiträge zur evangelischen Theologie, Band 287, 1959, pp. 345–50.) Hegel had also said that God was dead, namely the God of Church dogmatics. On this point cf. W. Anz, 'Tod und Unsterblichkeit' (in: *Einsichten*. Festschrift für G. Krüger, 1962, 11–35), p. 25. The 'atheism' of Hegel, however, is not nihilism in the sense of Jean Paul and Nietzsche.

[5] Heidegger, *Holzwege*, Frankfurt: Klostermann, 1950, 103–247. Cf. also Löwith, 'Nietzches antichristliche Bergpredigt', *Heidelberger Jahrbücher* 6, 1962, pp. 39–50.

the conviction that Western history has been determined for two thousand years by Greek metaphysics, through which the secularization of the world, brought to completion in modern times, has finally been established. We may here suspend judgement about the correctness of this assertion. Explicit atheism, in any case, is a phenomenon of the modern period, and Gerhard Ebeling has rightly said that this atheism is a counter-movement against Christianity.[1] It is also clear that the death of God for Nietzsche means the death of the Christian God. 'But', Heidegger adds, 'it is equally certain and is to be borne in mind in advance that the names of God and the Christian God are used to designate the supersensory world in general. God is the name for the realm of ideas and ideals.'[2]

The 'madman' cries: 'What did we do when we unchained this earth from its sun?', and continues: 'Where is it moving to now? Where are we moving to? Away from all suns? Do we not stumble all the time? Backwards, sidewards, forward, and in every direction? Is there an above and a below any more? Are we not wandering as through an endless nothingness?' The consequence of the death of God is therefore nihilism, as Jean Paul had pictured it.

We must guard against viewing *atheism* merely or even basically as a consequence of natural science and its world-view. To be sure, modern natural science has found the hypothesis 'God' unnecessary, according to the well-known dictum of La Place,[3] and the atheism of natural science has without doubt been widely influential, leading even to absurdities in Russia, where as the result of a space-flight it is given out that there was no trace of God in the space above the earth. Nevertheless, even when there are natural scientists today who again hold the hypothesis 'God' to be possible and appropriate, atheism is not thereby contradicted. For it has far deeper roots.

Atheism, as Jean Paul and Nietzsche understood it, is indeed nihilism, and this is not necessarily a consequence of the way in which natural science understands the world. In this respect the loss of the supernatural could be and was replaced

[1] G. Ebeling, *The Nature of Faith*, London, 1961, pp. 80 ff.; *Word and Faith*, London 1963, pp. 135 ff., 343.

[2] Heidegger, *Holzwege*, p. 199.

[3] Cf. Ebeling, *The Nature of Faith*, p. 81 f.

in the eighteenth and nineteenth centuries by the belief in progress and its accompanying optimism. The atheism of the natural sciences is a methodological procedure in so far as it subjects the world to an objectivizing way of viewing things. It must necessarily disregard God, because God, as the supersensory, cannot be the object of an objectivizing way of seeing.[1]

Atheism which ends in nihilism is rather the consequence of the *secularization of the world*, of which the objectivizing way of viewing nature is only a partial symptom. Secularization can be characterized simply as the world being conceived by man as an object[2] and thus delivered over to technology as its object.[3] This secularization takes place in every sphere of life, in morality, in law, in politics. For the relation of man to a transcendental power has been abandoned in all spheres of life. Heidegger calls this epoch in which the world has become an object the epoch of *subjectity*.[4] i.e., the era in which the world conceived as object is subjected to the planning of man as subject, a planning which is controlled by the values which man himself establishes.

And religion? One must first of all reflect that *Christianity itself was a decisive factor in the development of the secularization of the world* in that it de-divinized the world.[5] The Christian faith, by de-divinizing the world, allowed it to appear in its pure worldliness. It disclosed and evoked the *freedom*

[1] Op. cit.

[2] Cf. Heidegger, *Holzwege*, p. 236.

[3] Cf. Bonhoeffer, *Letters and Papers from Prison* (Fontana), p. 106 f.: 'Man has learned to cope with all questions of importance without recourse to God as a working hypothesis.' Also on the process of secularization, cf. Ebeling, *Word and Faith*, pp. 128 ff.; R. G. Smith, A Theological Perspective of the Secular, *The Christian Scholar*, 43, 1960, pp. 11–24, p. 18 f.

[4] Heidegger, *Holzwege*, p. 237. Subjectity, of course, is to be distinguished from subjectivity. The latter refers to the subjective mode of the individual in his judgements (e.g., judgements of taste); the former refers to the disposition of an entire epoch to the world and history, a disposition which has achieved the status of self-evidentness. [The reader will perhaps excuse the neologism subjectity, which represents Subjektität; the form is drawn by analogy: Subjektität—Subjektivität: subjectity—subjectivity. Trs.]

[5] Cf. Ebeling, *Word and Faith*, pp. 135 f., 344; *The Nature of Faith*, p. 80 f. Also especially F. Gogarten, *Verhängnis und Hoffnung der Neuzeit*, 1952; R. G. Smith, *A Theological Perspective*, p. 21.

of man from the world, freedom from all powers which can encounter man from out of the world.[1] It is the freedom of which Luther said: 'A Christian is a free master over all things and subject to no one.' This consciousness of freedom is the presupposition of the secularization of the world; the latter follows, however, only when the continuation of Luther's remark is forgotten: 'A Christian is a servant in the service of all things and subject to every one,' or, to put it differently, when it is forgotten that *freedom* from the world is at the same time *responsibility* for the world.[2] This forgetfulness increases the more man becomes conscious of the possibility, in pure objectivizing thought, of dominating the world through science and technology, of making it serve his purposes, values and plans.

This process plays the rôle, so to speak, which reason plays in life. Freedom from the world is at the same time responsibility for the world; that means, the world is delivered over to the reason of man.[3] For in order to be able to act responsibly, to come to decisions as they are required again and again, man must recognize the causal connexion of events in the world, must gain insight into causes and effects, and arrive at judgements about what serves the purpose and what does not. It is precisely for this purpose that he has his reason. Indeed, in the power of his reason he grasps the laws under which man's actions universally stand, i.e., the moral laws,

[1] Cf. Gogarten, op. cit., p. 8 (the most remarkable thing transpires in secularization) 'that the autonomy of man gains the radical sense which it has in the modern world only through the perceptions and experiences disclosed in the Christian faith'. Ibid., p. 12: Secularization is the 'legitimate consequence' of the Christian faith, and in so far as it 'is grounded in the Christian faith', it 'makes the world the world (Verweltlichung de Welt)'. Cf. ibid., pp. 93 ff.

[2] On the interdependence of freedom from the world and responsibility for the world, cf. Gogarten, op. cit., pp. 19, 24 ff. Vahanian makes the same point, *The Death of God*, p. 61: 'Biblical thought considers the world as man's sphere of action and pre-eminence. Man's responsibility to God and his involvement in the world emerge as polar elements attesting to the original goodness of creation.' It is significant that both Gogarten and Vahanian make the distinction between a legitimate secularization (secularity) and a denegerate secularism (secularism). Cf. Gogarten, p. 129 ff.; Vahanian, p. 60 ff. Cf. R. G. Smith, *A Theological Perspective*, p. 21.

[3] Cf. Gogarten, op. cit., p. 88.

whose force alone keeps the human community sound and whole. According to the myth of Protagoras in Plato,[1] Zeus sent reverence and justice to the earth by Hermes in order that political community might be possible. But rational judgements and plans, without which human work and community are not possible, are threatened by the danger that they will be placed in the service of self-seeking and that the authority of the moral laws will thereby wane.

The more reason is conscious of itself, the more the laws which regulate the community will no longer be simply derived from tradition, but will be understood as the moral laws which reason sanctions. And thus out of heteronomy arises *autonomy*. Autonomy is equivocal. In the genuine sense autonomy means self-legislation in the sense that the individual affirms the moral law as that in which he himself comes to win his authenticity.[2] But from the recognition that the rational man is a lawgiver in this sense, there arises the delusion that the individual as subject arbitrarily determines what is good and evil, as was the case already in the 'Greek Enlightenment' among the Sophists.[3] And so today autonomy is unfortunately often spoken of as a self-legislation of the individual, and that determines value and valuelessness of itself. The outcome is nihilism.[4]

[1] Plato, *Protagoras*, 322a–c.

[2] Cf. Kant, 'In this manner the moral law leads through the conception of the summum bonum, as the object and final end of pure practical reason, to religion, that is, to the recognition of all duties as divine commands, not as sanctions, that is to say, arbitrary ordinances of a foreign will and contingent in themselves, but as essential laws of every free will in itself, which, however, must be regarded as commands of the supreme being . . .' (Kant's *Critique of Practical Reason*, tr. T. K. Abbott, London: Longmans, 1923, p. 226.)

[3] Wandering Teachers who came to Athens in the 5th century B.C. (Ed.)

[4] On autonomy cf. also R. G. Smith, *A Theological Perspective*, p. 18. Ebeling puts it well in *Word and Faith*, p. 113 f.: 'But now, to the reality that concerns modern man there belongs . . . the discovery of the autonomy of the reason and accordingly the inescapable duty to make use of the autonomous reason—not, be it noted, to make autonomous use of the reason; for it is not man himself but reason which, rightly understood, is autonomous, whereas to confuse the autonomy of the reason with the autonomy of man results precisely in a new heteronomy of the reason . . .'

Religion was also drawn into the wake of 'subjectity'. That Christianity appears as a particular example of religion and is classified within the continuity of the history of religions (which, of course, is possible in any case) indicates that the decline has already set in. Moreover, if Christianity is acknowledged as the highest religion, then the capitulation to subjectity becomes evident at just that point. For the judgement about lower and higher religions can only be a judgement of the subject which evaluates. It is by no means the case that religion necessarily disappears in subjectity. If we consider the Western world, which has been a 'Christian' world for centuries, that world today is in general not anti-Christian, but a-Christian, partly in the sense that Christianity appears to it to be antiquated, and the questions to which Christianity proposes to give answers irrelevant; but partly in the sense that while the questions as such remain live issues, modern man himself now gives the answers. Thus ideologies arise, which assert that they are able to reveal the meaning of the world and history[1]; or doctrines of salvation are propagated, often from exotic religions, with the choice left to the subjectity of the individual; or again—especially in the U.S.A.—the biblical hope of a millennium is secularized, that is, converted into optimism which seeks to renew the world through the 'social gospel'.[2] But above all, there arises a religiosity to which men flee from the claims as well as from the bitterness or tediousness of secular everyday life.

'In the last analysis, religiosity is an expression of sublimated loneliness.'[3] The pressing problem for man in a world which has been cut loose from ties to the beyond is to find himself, to become certain of his own being. For with the loss of reference to the transcendent, man's certainty of knowledge concerning himself has also been lost.[4] The question of God does

---

[1] Cf. R. G. Smith, *A Theological Perspective*, p. 19.

[2] Cf. Vahanian, op. cit., p. 28 ff.

[3] Vahanian, op. cit., p. 4. Cf. also R. G. Smith, *A Theological Perspective*, p. 20 f.; *The New Man*, London, 1956, p. 62 f.

[4] Cf. Vahanian, op. cit., p. 183. Also, Bonhoeffer, LPP, p. 164: 'Man (scil. who is threatened by today's organization) is thrown back upon himself. He is ready to cope with everything, but not with himself. He is able to secure himself against everything, but not against man. In the last analysis, however, everything depends on man.' LPP., p. 178. Also, R. G. Smith, 'A Theological Perspective', p. 12.

not therefore die away; but the form of the question suggests
'that the deity is a missing link in man's unsuccessful attempts
to grasp the meaning of his self and of the world'.[1]

The question by no means completely dies away in decided
atheism either, provided that it draws back from the abyss of
nihilism and does not risk laying hold of the ideas of the transcendent God and his revelation, but would still like to speak
in some way of the divine as somehow immanent in the world,
whether it be as the world's creative ground or as the spiritual
life which lives and evolves in the world.[2] Indeed, one can say
that such 'atheism' stands nearer the Christian understanding
of faith than some institutional Christians who understand the
transcendent God as the beyond which has retired from the
world.[3]

Religiosity abandons precisely—at least according to the
Christian faith—that upon which genuine religion is based:
the relation of man to the transcendent God as that which
stands over against him. Religiosity thinks from the point of
view of the subjectivity of man. In this sense Karl Barth once
fought against Schleiermacher and the theology of experience
inaugurated by him, in which religion is understood as a pro-
vince of the human spirit, as the feeling of absolute dependence. To what extent Barth's criticism of Schleiermacher was
justified, I leave open.[4] In any case, it was justified to the
extent that the relation to God was reduced to feeling. Vahanian takes up this battle against religiosity from the standpoint of the Christian faith with renewed vigour, as did
Bonhoeffer before him. And they are followed by John
Robinson.

Gone is *the relation of man to the transcendent* as that which
stands over against man and the world and is not at their

[1] Vahanian, op. cit., p. 78.

[2] Cf., for example, what Robinson, op. cit., pp. 127–9, says about
Julian Huxley and Albert Camus.

[3] It is therefore understandable when Robinson, p. 127, produces a
variation on Paul's formulation for 1 Corinthians 9:20 f.: 'I am prepared to be an agnostic with the agnostic, even an atheist with the
atheists.' Likewise, cf. R. G. Smith, *The New Man*, p. 109, on Feuer-
bach.

[4] On this point cf. C. Senft, *Wahrhaftigkeit und Wahrheit*. Die
Theologie des 19. Jahrhunderts zwischen Orthodoxie und Aufklärung
(Beiträge zur historischen Theologie, 22), 1956, pp. 1–46.

disposal, which is manifested only through encounter, only as gift, and cannot be reached by turning away from the world in a religious flight into a beyond. Now the word transcendence is ambiguous. It can be said that rational thought transcends all unmethodical and random thought. Reason is transcendent with respect to primitive-innocent opinions as well as arbitrary individual judgements and evaluations. But reason remains in the sphere of subjectivity, while religion, particularly the Christian faith, abandons this sphere.[1] The Christian faith speaks of a revelation, by which it understands God's act as an event which is not visible to the objectivizing thought of reason, an event which does not communicate doctrines, but concerns the existence of man[2] and teaches him, or better, enables him to understand himself as sustained by the transcendent power of God.[3]

In this, theologians like Tillich, Bonhoeffer, Ebeling, Vahanian, R. G. Smith and Robinson are one. But they are also agreed that *the transcendent* is to be sought and can be found not above or beyond the world, but *in the midst of this world*.[4]

[1] I leave it open here whether and to what extent it can be said that the existential life (e.g., in personal relationships) transcends the sphere of subjectivity.

[2] Here I disregard the paradox, which involves the revelatory event being at once an historical as well as an eschatological event, both with respect to its origin, Jesus Christ, and with respect to its constant renewal in the church's proclamation.

[3] If one is persuaded that every man is basically moved by the question of God and that therefore the Christian proclamation may reckon with a pre-understanding, then one can ask whether this pre-understanding is not also concealed precisely in religiosity. Now H. G. Gadamer, in his book, *Wahrheit und Methode* (Tübingen: Siebeck, 1960), which is of greatest significance for theologians, has contested (in the context of the hermeneutical problem, p. 313 f.) whether one can speak of a pre-understanding for the understanding of the biblical texts, namely, a pre-understanding that is given with the question of God that drives human existence. I am of the opinion that the pre-understanding is given precisely in that experience which Gadamer designates as the 'authentic experience', namely, the experience in which 'man becomes conscious of his finiteness' (p. 339 f.). This experience is certainly not always realized, but it surely persists as an ever-present possibility.

[4] For R. G. Smith cf. *A Theological Perspective*, p. 15; *The New Man*, pp. 65–70, and especially pp. 94–112: 'This-Worldly Transcendance'. Ebeling, *The Nature of Faith*, p. 160 f.

Allow me to quote some sentences of Bonhoeffer: 'The "beyond" of God is not the beyond of our cognitive faculties. Epistemological transcendence has nothing to do with the transcendence of God. God is transcendent in the midst of our life.' The transcendent is not the infinitely remote, but the nearest at hand.'[1] The 'death of God', according to Vahanian, takes place precisely in that the transcendent presence of God is lost if transcendence is conceived as purely other-worldly—just as in religiosity.' Or, to quote another formulation of Vahanian: 'Religious authority does not entail the eradication of personal autonomy for the sake of blind assent to a system of beliefs claiming sanction of absolute or divine authority. But religious authority . . . symbolizes a synthesis of subjective truth and objective reality . . . Faith is an attempt to reconcile subject and object, subjective truth and objective reality, without overwhelming either one of the terms.'[3]

Faith permits the world to be the world; indeed, it gives back to the world its authentic worldliness; faith 'recognizes the hidden unconditional ground even in the most autonomous of human pursuits. It needs to welcome those pursuits not for the hope that they may be violently "baptized" into Christ, but for their own sake'.[4] Dietrich Bonhoeffer formulates the discernment of faithful relation to the world very pointedly: 'And we cannot be honest without recognizing that we must live in the world—*etsi deus non daretur*. And this is just what we

[1] LPP, pp. 165, 163. On Bonhoeffer cf. especially R. G. Smith, *The New Man*, pp. 96–106; Ebeling, 'The Non-religious Interpretation of Biblical Concepts', in *Word and Faith*, pp. 98–161.

[2] Vahanian, op. cit., p. 44.

[3] Op. cit., p. 164 f. Cf. II; 'Now, as then, today and always, the Christian problem is to correlate the truth of Christianity with the empirical truths men live by, without confusing them: man cannot live by one or the other kind of truth alone,' p. 169: 'On the contrary, even as the meaning of existence lies outside existence, in the dialectical relatedness implied by the polarity between Creator and creature, so also the meaning of history lies above and beyond history.' The formulation of Tillich, quoted also by Vahanian, is in substantial agreement: 'Theology moves back and forth between two poles, the eternal truth of its foundation and the temporal situation in which the eternal truth must be received' (*Systematic Theology*, Vol. I, Chicago University Press, 1951, p. 3).

[4] R. G. Smith, *The New Man*, p. 69.

do recognize—before God! God himself drives us to this recognition.'[1] This is precisely what Robinson designates as the necessary revolution: the God above the world having become the God beyond the world, today it is a question of finding God in the midst of the world, in the present. The contrast between here and beyond, and thus the contrast between naturalism and supernaturalism, must be overcome. God must be recognized as the unconditional in the conditional.

It is surprising how such theological perceptions are also taken up by sociologists. Eckart Schleth says in his book, *Der profane Weltchrist*: 'The unity of Christ and world is found in the "nevertheless" of the believer for the world, in his imperceptible eschatological existence here and now, in his freedom from the world, in the world and for the world.' Also 'Life in faith, the character of which is to be permanently in process of fulfilment, is life in the "ultimate reality", which is always here and now and identical with everyday things.'[2]

The relation of faith and worldliness is a dialectical relationship, as R. G. Smith especially has emphasized.[3] I will try to make the meaning of this dialectical relation clear by means of an analogy. The loving look into an eye which is loved and loving is fundamentally different from the objectivizing look with which an ophthalmologist examines the eye of a patient. But when the doctor who has to treat the diseased eye is also the one who loves, the two ways of seeing stand in a dialectical relationship; he has to examine the eye of the other in an objectivizing way precisely in his love. The objectivizing way of seeing enters into the service of the one who loves. Robinson endeavours, following Tillich, to make clear the relation between faith and worldliness in the dialectical relation between engagement with the world and withdrawal from the world. To this dialectic corresponds the dialectic in the relation of man to God, namely, as the relation between

---

[1] *Letters and Papers from Prison*, pp. 121 ff. (see Vol. 5, pp. 87 ff)
[2] E. Schleth, *Der profane Weltchrist*. Neubau der Lebensform für den Industriemenschen, 1957, pp. 114, 159. Cf. p. 8: The author is of the opinion 'that the church as "eschatological phenomenon" occurs where Christians without reservation take the profane world seriously, because only in the "solidarity of faith and unfaith" can the new creation in Christ be recognized and the world served by it'.
[3] *The New Man*, pp. 106 ff., also pp. 58–70.

personal freedom and utter dependence, between ultimacy and intimacy.[1]

He who has understood the dialectic of the relationship between worldliness and faith in relation to the transcendent God, also sees that the recognition of God as the nearest at hand, as he who is in the midst of worldly life, does not imply pantheism.[2] For the dialectic is missing in pantheism, and it avoids the paradox that is given to man to conquer by grasping the unconditional in the conditional in every now: that means, not in a theory, but in existential comportment, in the conscious or unconscious decisions of life.

The contrast can be made clear by saying that faith in the transcendent presence of God can be expressed in the phrase 'transformations of God'. Ernst Barlach chose this phrase in order to say that the paradox of the presence of God in the world takes shape in ever new form, just as God himself wishes to give expression to the supra-real and infinite in his works perpetually in new forms.

Ernst Troeltsch once also spoke of the 'transformations of God', since he sought to hold on to the idea of God in his philosophy of history in view of the 'pluralism of reality and its movement' *vis-à-vis* changes in the knowledge of truth and ideals.[3] These changes depend upon an 'inner life-knowledge of the All or the Divinity', upon a 'life-process of the Absolute', a 'becoming of the divine Spirit'.

Troeltsch saw the problem, but he sought to solve it not on the basis of the historicity (*Geschichtlichkeit*) of human existence, but from a standpoint which views history from the outside and speculatively postulates a transcendent deity, which always has its life beyond my historicity.[4]

Hans Jonas represents the opposite extreme in his essay 'Immortality and the Modern Temper',[5] in which he projects,

[1] Robinson, op. cit., pp. 100, 130 f.

[2] R. G. Smith, *A Theological Perspective*, p. 16, also emphasizes this point.

[3] E. Troeltsch, *Der Historismus und seine Probleme*, 1922. The formulations in question, to which reference is made above, are collected by Gogarten, *Verhängnis und Hoffnung der Neuzeit*, pp. 112–14.

[4] For criticism of Troeltsch, see Gogarten, op. cit., pp. 114–16.

[5] *Harvard Theological Review*, 55, 1962, pp. 1–20.

so to speak, the historicity of man into God himself and speaks of the destiny of the deity for which man is responsible.[1] We men are experiments of eternity, as it were, and God's own destiny is at stake in our decisions, in the universe to which he has given himself up. God's being at the mercy of the world does not mean his immanence in the sense of pantheism. Rather, there is the paradox that the deity has chosen a destiny which consists in the continuous elevation out of immanence into transcendence, for which we men are responsible. In such a process, in the succession of surrender and deliverance, the deity becomes itself.

Schubert M. Ogden understands God's being as historical being in another way.[2] God's eternity is not to be conceived as his timelessness following the metaphysical tradition, but rather as his eminent temporality, his historicity.[3] God is a God who acts, as he is known in the Bible; his self must therefore be conceived in strict analogy with the human self, and anthropological language about God is entirely appropriate. Just as man is not an isolated I, neither is God. Without the universe, without the world, his creation, God is not. To this extent he not only stands in relation to the world, but is dependent upon it. But this dependence is actual, i.e., it is actualized in his own free decisions as well as in the free decisions, which correspond to his own, of the creatures that constitute his world. Decisions arising from the unbounded love as answer to God themselves contribute to God's self-creation.

This all certainly sounds astonishing at first hearing. For is not God, as we learned from Psalm 90, he who was there before the mountains were brought forth and the earth and the world created, God from everlasting to everlasting? Indeed he is ! But we understand Ogden when we comprehend

[1] Jonas, of course, also sees the dialectic between the relation to the world and the relation to God, and says that we encounter the eternal in the temporal, especially in the decisions in which eternity and nothingness meet in one in that the now of the decision is always to be understood as the final moment of time granted us. That means in fact to understand the end in a light from beyond time.

[2] *Journal of Religion*, 43, 1963, pp. 1–19.

[3] Cf. M. Heidegger, *Being and Time*, tr. J. Macquarrie and E. Robinson, London, 1962, 499, n. xiii: 'If God's eternity can be "construed" philosophically, then it may be understood only as a more primordial temporality which is "infinite".'

how he endeavours to free the idea of the eternity of God from the metaphysical conception of God as the unmoved mover, the *causa sui*,[1] and to conceive the eternity of God as historical without giving up thinking of God as creator. If, according to the biblical tradition, God is a person, so is he historical. In support of the view that God is not, apart from the world, the creator is not, apart from the creation, Ogden is able to invoke John 1 : 1–3, that remarkable assertion that in the beginning was the word, and the word of creation at that, through which everything came into being. This word in the beginning was with God, indeed the word was God. That is no different from what Ogden intends to say. And when we reflect on the word 'before' in the psalm, it is to be said that already for the psalmist the meaning of 'before' is not exhausted in the chronological sense, but that it means the creative superiority, the creative origin. This origin did not occur once as *prima causa*, out of which world history then unfolded in time; on the contrary, the origin is always present.

With this we come back to the assertion that for modern man the idea of God above or beyond the world is either no longer viable or is distorted into a religiosity which would like to escape from the world. By no means ! Only the idea of God which finds, which can seek and find, the unconditional in the conditional, the beyond in the here, the transcendent in the present at hand, as possibility of encounter, is possible for modern man.

It then remains to keep oneself open at any time for the *encounter with God in the world, in time*. It is not the acknowledgement of an image of God, be it ever so correct, that is real faith in God; rather, it is the readiness for the eternal to encounter us at any time in the present—at any time in the varying situations of our life. Readiness consists in openness in allowing something really to encounter us that does not leave the I alone, the I that is encapsulated in its purposes and plans, but whose encounter transforms us, permits us to become new selves again and again. The situation can be heartening just as well as disheartening, can be challenging as

[1] Cf. M. Heidegger, *Identität und Differenz*, 1957, p. 70 f. (Essays in Metaphysics: Identity and Difference, tr. Kurt F. Leidecker, New York: Philosophical Library, 1960, p. 64 f.)

well as requiring endurance. What is demanded is selflessness, not as a pattern of moral behaviour, but as the readiness not to cling to our old selves, but to receive our authentic selves ever anew. This can be a questioning readiness, but it can also be completely unconscious. For, suprisingly, God can encounter us where we do not expect it.[1]

We have thus perhaps come to an understanding of what is meant by the 'transformations of God'. All of us are probably acquainted with sagas and legends, pagan as well as Christian, in which the profound idea of the transformation of God has been concealed in the mythological representation of the metamorphosis of the deity or of gods, who visit a mortal incognito and unrecognized. How the one visited receives the god determines his destiny.

The New Testament contains the most striking proclama-

[1] That is evidently also the intention of Herbert Braun, whose avoidance of the word 'God' in his delineation of what the New Testament has to say to me (*Gesammelte Studien zum Neuen Testament und seiner Umwelt*, Tübingen: Siebeck, 1962, p. 297) has offended and evoked criticism (cf. especially H. Gollwitzer, *Die Existenz Gottes im Bekenntnis des Glaubens*, 1963, pp. 26–9). Braun's purpose is to emphasize, over against atheism with a world-view, that God is not 'the one who exists for himself', but rather is 'the whence of my being driven around' (op. cit., p. 341). This being driven about is understood by Braun as determined by the 'I may' and 'I ought'. It might be asked how this dialectic (if it may be called that) relates to the dialectic between worldliness and a believing relation to transcendence. But, in any case, the relation to transcendence is understood in the New Testament, according to Braun, as an event, and indeed, as he formulates it, as an 'unexpectable' event (p. 275). The believing self-understanding awakened in such an event is not theoretical knowledge, but 'an event which occurs again and again' (p. 277). The truth of the relation to transcendence understood in this sense is 'bound to its being perpetually proclaimed anew' (p. 277) and to its being heeded (p. 297), to its being heard (p. 298), respectively. The self-understanding awakened by such hearing is actualized in concrete human community. Braun is thus able to put it very sharply: 'Man as man, man in his community with man, implies God.'—R. G. Smith also emphasizes the importance of the community, *A Theological Perspective*, p. 22: 'Man is (scil. man) in so far as he receives. He is (scil. man) only so far as he is whole. And this wholeness is found only in relation to others. Man's being is being in relation. This simply cannot be arranged or planned. It happens, it is an event in which man's being is disclosed in the presence of the other.' The problem of the relation of law and gospel also belongs here; see, e.g., Ebeling, *Word and Faith*, p. 143 f.

tions of the 'transformations' of God, and oddly enough in the picture which Jesus sketches of the last judgement (Matt. 25: 31–46). The Judge of the world assembles all men before his throne, some to the right, some to the left. To those on the right he says: 'I was hungry and you gave me food, I was thirsty and you gave me drink, I was a stranger and you welcomed me...' And when those so addressed inquire in astonishment, 'When did we do all this ?', the Lord will answer, 'What you did to one of the least of these my brethren you did to me !' The dialogue with those on the left runs correspondingly 'I was hungry and you me no food, I was thirsty and you gave me no drink...' And when they ask, 'Lord, when did we see thee hungry or thirsty... and did not minister to thee ?', then they must face the answer, 'What you did not do to the least of these, you did not do to me either !' This picture thus contains the two doctrines which belong together, of the 'transformations' of God and of the presence of eternity in time.

(FROM: *World Come of Age*, A symposium on Dietrich Bonhoeffer, edited by R. Gregor Smith, London 1967, pp. 256–73.)

FOR FURTHER STUDY AND DISCUSSION

1 The debate about the results of form-criticism and its bearing on the question of the historical Jesus continues. A volume of essays critical of Bultmann's handling of form-criticism and suggesting a number of questions for further study is *Vindications* (edited by Anthony Hanson) 1966. Professor Dennis Nineham has replied to some of the criticisms made there in an essay published in *Christian History and Interpretation* (Essays presented to John Knox) edited by W. R. Farmer, C. F. D. Moule and R. R. Niebuhr, 1968.

2 Is the 'demythologizing' enterprise necessary and worth-

while? Some critical questions raised by Bultmann's work will be found in an appendix on 'demythologizing' in Hugo Meynell's *Sense, nonsense and Christianity* 1964 and also in his *The New Theology and Modern Theologians* 1967.

FOR FURTHER READING

PRINCIPAL WORKS OF RUDOLF BULTMANN
(in English translation)

'The Study of the Synoptic Gospels' in *Form Criticism* edited by F. C. Grant, 1962, New York (Harper Torchbooks).

Jesus and the Word (translated by L. P. Smith and E. Huntress), London (Fontana Books), 1962.

Theology of the New Testament (translated by Kendrick Grobel), Vol. I, 1952; Vol. II, 1955, London.

'New Testament and Mythology', 'A reply to the theses of Julius Schniewind', 'Bultmann replies to his critics' in *Kerygma and Myth*, Vol. I (edited by H.-W. Bartsch), London, 1953.

Jesus Christ and Mythology, London, 1960.

History and Eschatology, New York (Harper Torchbooks), 1962.

Existence and Faith (shorter writings selected, translated and introduced by Schubert M. Ogden), Fontana Books, London, 1964.

SOME BOOKS ABOUT RUDOLF BULTMANN

L. Malevez, *The Christian Message and Myth*: the theology of Rudolf Bultmann, London, 1958. (A very valuable critique of Bultmann by a Roman Catholic theologian.)

Paul Althaus, *The so-called kerygma and the historical Jesus*, Edinburgh, 1959. (An excellent discussion of the place of history and the historical Jesus in Bultmann's theology.)

David Cairns, *A gospel without myth?* London, 1960.

John Macquarrie, *The scope of demythologizing*, London, 1960.
H. A. Meynell, *The New Theology and Modern Theologians*, London, 1967. (A stimulating volume of essays containing some shrewd comments on Bultmann's theological method.)

FOR GENERAL BACKGROUND READING

John Macquarrie, *Twentieth-century Religious Thought*, 1963.
——, *God-talk*, 1967.
——, *God and Secularity*, 1968.
Frederick Ferré, *Language, Logic and God*, 1962.
——, *Basic Modern Philosophy of Religion*, 1968.
David E. Jenkins, *Guide to the Debate about God*, 1966.
Colin Williams, *Faith in a Secular Age*, 1966.
E. L. Mascall, *The Secularisation of Christianity*, 1965.
H. Gollwitzer, *The Existence of God as confessed by faith*, 1964.
A. M. Ramsey, *God, Christ and the World*, 1969.
T. W. Ogletree, *The Death of God Controversy*, 1966.